CCCC Studies in Writing & Rhetoric

DIGITAL GRIOTS

DIGITAL GRIOTS

AFRICAN AMERICAN RHETORIC IN A MULTIMEDIA AGE

Adam J. Banks

Southern Illinois University Press
Carbondale and Edwardsville

14 13 12 11   4 3 2 1

Publication partially funded by a subvention grant from the Conference on College Composition and Communication of the National Council of Teachers of English.

Library of Congress Cataloging-in-Publication Data
  Banks, Adam J. (Adam Joel)
  Digital griots : African American rhetoric in a multimedia age / Adam J. Banks.
      p. cm. — (CCCC studies in writing & rhetoric)
  Includes bibliographical references and index.
  ISBN-13: 978-0-8093-3020-1 (pbk. : alk. paper)
  ISBN-10: 0-8093-3020-2 (pbk. : alk. paper)
  ISBN-13: 978-0-8093-8619-2 (ebook)
  ISBN-10: 0-8093-8619-4 (ebook)
  1. African Americans—Communication. 2. English language—United States—Rhetoric. 3. African Americans—Intellectual life. 4. Oratory—United States. 5. Black English. I. Title.
  P94.5.A37B36 2010
  302.2089'96073—dc22   2010019998

The paper used in this publication meets the minimum requirements of American National Standard for Information Sciences—Permanence of Paper for Printed Library Materials, ANSI Z39.48-1992. ∞

CONTENTS

ACKNOWLEDGMENTS

Thanks first and always to my mentor, Keith Gilyard, for giving composition a vision of its theoretical work and teaching rooted in the dogged pursuit of social justice and of practice built on the balance of searing critique and soaring celebration. Dr. G, bka Geneva Smitherman, you continue to be the model of what we're all trying to do in the academy. Much, much love to you for your courage and rawness in showing the rest of us the way. To Joe Harris, SWR series editor, I am also grateful for the excitement you showed for this project from its earliest versions and for the thoughtful feedback he has given at various stages of its development. To Kristine Priddy and many others on the staff of Southern Illinois University Press, you have been wonderfully diligent and professional in helping to prepare the manuscript for publication. To Beverly Moss and Morris Young, much thanks for the serious, engaged reads you gave the proposal and manuscript and for your many helpful suggestions that strengthened the final version. I also owe my colleagues at Syracuse University, particularly Eileen Schell and Gwendolyn Pough, a real debt of gratitude for their encouragement as they read late versions of the manuscript. Several of the strong graduate students at SU have also influenced this project: Elisa Norris, Tamika Carey, Derek Mueller, and Denise Valdes, you each have great gifts to give the academy. Keep pushin, keep pennin.

But beyond the wisdom in her serious reading and review of the manuscript, Beverly Moss has it right: sometimes a community text does indeed arise. To the extent that this project meets any of its goals, much of the credit must go to members of Syracuse's black community who met together and shared ideas and fellowship over six years of courses, workshops, symposia, forums, meals, and many other activities. The dialogue we shared from The Groove and the Dunbar Center to the Paul Robeson Performing Arts Center and SU's campus not only sustained and strengthened me but helped me to see even more clearly that intellectual work must make our collective claims of and desires for community engagement real—not through official programs but by getting off campus and actually engaging and being engaged. Community literacy work must be about community even more than about literacy itself and must begin with the beauty, power, and agency of the communities we enter and the people we hope to build with. So many people have helped shape this book and my own vision as it has developed over the last several years. Chuck Jones, this all began with you, bro. I'm glad to have you as my right hand. Thanks for all the time you spent spinning these ideas, and thanks even more for your friendship.

Ife Nellons, Lorraine Ford, Kookie Harley, and Angel Howze—you all brought so much life, and fun, and challenge to this work, and I'm forever grateful for your major contributions, from The Groove all the way to today. Jackie Grace Rasheed and Jawwaad Rasheed, you are both amazing examples of serious intellectual commitment at work in service of the people. Keep shining your light so I can see. Gloria and George Kilpatrick, the couple bringing new inspiration far beyond the radio show, thank you for your friendship and advice. Don the "Harlem Son" and LaToya "Ms. Pat" Sawyer, aka Kindred, aka Peaches and Herb, you both guided the vision and the activities of these last six years. Thank you so much for your inspiration and "fiyah." Janet Bennett and Karen Stanislaus Fung, thanks for all those trips you took down the Thruway; you were both serious parts of the glue that brought us and held us all together. Linda Littlejohn and Langston McKinney, you keep reminding us all that it's about the work, it's about the people. Brilliant, wise, and committed—and straight up real—I'm so glad to have been able to connect with and learn from you. So many others deserve mention here, but for all of those who have been a part of the classes, the

Saturday Academy, the forums, and other activities, I appreciate you so much. You have shown me other ways to think about scholarship and intellectual work.

To everyone, named and unnamed, who has been a part of the journey of this book project and my overall development as a scholar during this time at Syracuse, you bring models and a vision that I'm still reaching for. I hope you keep working with me and working on me and that you find something here that reflects and is worth all you've given me.

DIGITAL GRIOTS

Scratch: Two Turntables and a Storytelling Tradition

DJing is Writing/Writing is DJing. . . . But there's something about the labor of writing and the sense of being part of the continuum of writing that goes back thousands of years. It is an ancient form, and in some ways it doesn't quite fit what is happening. The challenge then is to describe or characterize what it feels like to be alive now in the midst of it, but using this form of communication. . . . Saying that people are literate means that they have read widely enough to reference texts, to put them in a conceptual framework. They are capable of creating an overview. This kind of literacy exists in the musical arena, too. The more you have heard, the easier it is to find links and to recognize quotations. . . . Writing becomes your own temple and you just move in and make sure everything flows and the right divinities are in effect. It's a puzzle you set for yourself. Being at a crossroads and questioning how far to push writing, or music, or art, uncertain which direction to move, is actually a good thing, because it forces me to go back to the basic issues. Why do I want to write?
—Paul D. Miller, Rhythm Science

THE SCRATCH IS AN INTERRUPTION. It breaks the linearity of the text, the progressive circularity of the song. It takes the listener or reader back and forth through the song, underneath the apparatus that plays it, either to insert some other song or for the sheer pleasure of the sound of the scratch itself. What was noise, what was seen as the sign of a broken record or stylus, an unwelcome interruption in the continual march of text, groove, history, became a purposeful interruption, became pleasurable, became a way to insert other voices in a text, to redirect one's attention. It is difficult to overstate just how much the scratch changed music, how crucial it was to the brash announcement that Hip Hop did indeed come to change the game and even attempt to change the world. This book looks to scratch, to interrupt, to play a while in the grooves of two records—disciplinary conversations about African American rhetoric and those about multimedia writing—to begin to blend and loop them while posing one question: how can African American rhetorical traditions and practices inform composition's current endeavors to define, theorize, and practice multimedia writing? To put it differently, in a moment when many compositionists have identified the mix and remix as tropes for digital writing practices—to the point of arguing, as Johndan Johnson-Eilola and Stuart Selber have, that we live and write in a "remix culture"—what might we learn from the rhetorical practices and traditions of the culture that gave us the remix? The short answer that this book proposes is that DJ Kool Herc, Afrika Bambaataa, and legions and lineages of other DJs, including Beth Coleman, DJ Spooky, Kid Capri, Grand Wizard Theodore, Biz Markie, Grandmaster Flash, Juan Atkins, Spindarella, and thousands more, are responsible for the conceptual framework that forms our response to the challenges of digital, multimedia writing. For all of our academic affection for citing major theorists to remind us that everyday practices by everyday people construct the cultures that we come later to study, the African American DJ in the Hip Hop tradition (a tradition that was nurtured by a long history of the black radio DJ, with figures like Al Benson, Jack Cooper, Cathy Hughes, and Petey Greene as well as Lady Skill and Jeffrey Charles in my hometown of Cleveland) lived theory and created writing practices that helped make postmodern conceptions of writing possible.

Beyond charting the early 1970s parties in the Bronx where Clive Campbell, aka DJ Kool Herc, looped copies of the same song together on two turntables in order to isolate and stretch out the "break" as an originary moment for our current understandings of writing in a multimedia age and calling for more scholarly attention to the black discursive and rhetorical traditions and practices surrounding the work of the DJ, I also argue that the DJ provides the figure through whom African American rhetoric can be reimagined in a new century. Understanding the DJ as a current manifestation of the griot—as a digital griot—and linking the practices of the DJ to other griots throughout the tradition (the storytellers, the preachers, the standup comics, the spoken word poets, and others) will allow an approach to African American rhetoric that is fluid and forward looking yet firmly rooted in African traditions. The exemplary DJ is a model of rhetorical excellence, and even the everyday DJ is often a model of real rhetorical agility. A canon maker. A time binder. A model of the Gramscian organic intellectual at work, the intellectual who is nurtured and sustained by local communities rather than professionalized in universities or think tanks or foundations. Building a context for theorizing digital, multimedia writing and literacies from the everyday practices of African Americans in this way allows us to extend Antonio Gramsci's concept of the organic intellectual beyond the individual figure into collective organic intellectual work. But let me cut to how I might put it in a different context, a less academic description of the DJ as digital griot and what this figure offers our conceptions of writing and rhetoric:

> standing between tradition and future, holding the power to shape how both are seen/heard/felt/known. exhibiting mastery of techniques, but always knowing that techniques carry stories, arguments, ways of viewing the world, that the techniques arrange the texts, that every text carries even more stories, arguments, epistemologies.

> analyzing audiences their wants their needs their knowledges their attitudes joys pains fears—in any given situation—at a moment's notice. holding the crowd in the palm of one's hands, on the tips of her fingers. always on some new ish technology cut song line break but always understanding the importance of knowing traditions, always searching always questioning always researching digging in the crates looking for that cut that break that connection nobody else has found, nobody else has used quite that way. practicing her craft constantly.

bearer of history, memory, and rememory, able to turn on the planetary or intergalactic time space transporter within seconds. interpreting a world, implicitly and explicitly telling us how to manage the madness of it all, how to live in it but still escape with our souls. always in conversation with too many audiences, but always with an answer, as temporary as it must be, always layering the multiple responses to them all at all times. personality. voice. flow. being expected to have your own style, your own flow, your own technique(s), even as you're expected to know the conversation, know the tradition, shape and reshape them. disrupting the line/text/narrative/argument/worldview/world to recreate all through the arrangement. the ultimate individual artist, but every bit as much owned by the community. the producer. shaping relationships helping the lover fighter organizer grassroots worker politician rapper MC say what they can't quite reach/feel. translating bigger movements working the code to make sure your peoples understand it but the overseers, the panopticon, don't.

blowing someone's mind—oh my damn he didn't just put that on top of that! bring that beat back! bearer of ritual. master of ceremonies. remixing more than songs, more than narratives—repurposing old technologies and new and remixing social economic political intimate relationships. recreating a world again. again old, again, new. always with a plan but always improvising, in the moment. be the entrepreneur, or work the club, the station, or both/all? what do my peoples need from me? the first rapper before there were rappers. what do i have to say? holding sequencing shaping individual and collective memory. constantly juggling not just beats but ethical questions and commitments and responsibilities—am i satisfied with freakin a short playlist that i know will move the crowd, get me some applause, get me that grade? do i use my craft to get the most money possible—is it really CREAM? or do i keep pushing, looking for boundaries to break, continually searching for something new to connect with the old, for that old/new way to create another world, another universe, another text?

cut break mix scratch bootleg remix layer mixtape loop fade call and response signifyin pastiche move the crowd enter the conversation change the game own your own take them *there*.

Between tradition and future. The ways in which racial inequalities are calcified in twenty-first-century America, hardened in the veins of our society, even as there is less and less room in public discourse and policy work for either redress or even honest dialogue, call us to a repositioning, a different way of seeing the relationships between tradition and future in the shaping of new approaches to present challenges and possibilities. In the pursuit of greater equality in our education system, from K to PhD, technology access, print literacies, and verbal skill all collide as requirements for even basic participation in an information-based, technology-dependent economy and society. The health of cities and regions still reeling from forty years of deindustrialization demands such a repositioning. The exorbitant expense of a narrow strategy of importing technical talent from abroad while refusing to invest in it at home demands it. The continued inequality in our education system demands it. The growing role of an evolving digital divide in shaping young people's educational futures demands it. Technology and education collide with and exacerbate long-standing inequalities to such an extent that we must rethink old narratives to have any chance at addressing either our old problems or the new ones that will compound them. Any attempt to foster meaningful access to communication technologies or to a working education system must include theoretical frameworks or conceptual models that build from the traditions and truths of a people and assume their agency and ability. Black people must see themselves in the digital story.

Just as black communities are lining up new tracks to match our current realities, African American rhetoric as an area of study and composition as a discipline are also in great need of repositioning or, as Alondra Nelson would describe it, synchronizing of traditional narratives and futuristic visions. When it comes to discussions of race, ethnicity, and culture in multimedia writing, both the lack of scholars of color in the discussion and the paucity of attention to the actual practices and conceptual frameworks that African American, Latino/a, Indigenous, and Chicano/a traditions could bring to the discussion demonstrate that we are still writing in the spaces jacked as well as writing in the spaces left. And while scholarship in African American rhetoric has grown tremendously from contributions by a generation 2.0, those of us in that 2.0 need that same synchronizing Nelson calls for. The group I identify as generation 2.0 of African American scholars in the discipline includes a wide range of early- and mid-career scholars like Gwendolyn Pough, Vershawn Young, David Holmes, Aesha Adams, David Kirkland, Vorris Nunley, and many more who entered the academy after Bill Cook's classic 1993 article "Writing in the Spaces Left" and who built their work on that of groundbreaking figures like Cook, Geneva Smitherman, Jacqueline Jones Royster, and Keith Gilyard. For all of the important work this crew has placed in the disciplinary conversation, collectively we are still woefully short of engagements with technology, with Elaine Richardson, Carmen Kynard, and Samantha Blackmon being the main scholars stepping up to this major issue of our time. Generation 2.0 in the African American rhetoric game needs an old school/new school mixtape, a new, repositioned conception of the field and our work within it that continues the trajectories charted by the generation that brought us from Students' Right to Spaces Left. While I will outline in the conclusion what an African American rhetoric 2.0 might look like, let me just say here that such a remix, or re-vision, of the field would lead us to a new theoretical approach that remains just as firmly grounded in the contributions of the scholars who opened up space for us to have a chance to be valued in the writing classroom, to get into PhD programs and into the academy and scholarly conversation, while committing itself equally to addressing the problems and possibilities of writing in a multimedia age.

In some ways, I'm issuing a similar call to the one that defined my initial study of African American rhetoric in *Race, Rhetoric, and*

Technology: Searching for Higher Ground. In this case, however, I have shifted from using James Brown and Parliament-Funkadelic's concept of The One—as the embodiment of a theoretical approach to African American rhetoric to allow for both unity and diversity and a focus on both black communities and dialogue with all members of our society—to one that examines the figure who has kept funk alive through the cut, break, scratch, sample, mix, remix, and mixtape in order to read those rhetorical practices and their attendant traditions more closely so that they might better inform future composition and African American rhetoric theory, teaching, and practice. Of course, funk and the DJ do not make up an either/or choice: P-Funk, James Brown, and the DJ are merely different instantiations of the "groove" that allows Alexander G. Weheliye to link writing, orality, and technology: "Instead of emphasizing either the technological or the cultural, the grooves of sonic Afro-modernity integrate both" (16).

I should be clear here that this project is not a history of the DJ, nor an analysis of important DJs in the tradition or classic sets, mixes, remixes, or mixtapes. And while this work is grounded in a concern for rhetoric in what, following Weheliye and Joel Dinerstein in what might be termed a black techno-dialogic tradition, it is not a project on persuasion in digital spaces like one might find from Barbara Warnick's influential book *Rhetoric Online* or from Johnson-Eilola's *Datacloud* or my colleague Collin Brooke's *Lingua Franca*. Instead, I use the theoretical or conceptual work that the mix, remix, and mixtape do as lenses or ways to contextualize my study of a wide range of black multimedia rhetorical practices. So the chapters here cohere and yet they don't; they flow and yet they cut to other tracks, other conversations, looping in other voices in what might seem to be idiosyncratic ways. Some quotes get looped repeatedly, to serve a function like that of the sample—foundational ideas I borrow and build on that are too important for a single reference. And the prose itself spins, develops in circular ways at times, working through layering and repetition as well as through linear argument. In those ways, I hope this book models the mix and remix and becomes a kind of mixtape of its own, taking me back to the days of recording slow jams from Jeffrey Charles and WZAK 93.1's "For Lovers Only" and bomb Hip Hop tracks from Johnny O and Cochise on WDMT 107.9's "Club Style," trying to get all of the song without cutting it off or inadvertently picking up a commercial or conversation, and takes composition and African American rhetoric forward for readers to create their own tracks, mixes, and mixtapes in the conversation.

The chapters that follow continue to make the case for an approach to African American rhetoric that synchronizes oral traditions, print, and digital writing as well as the dialectic tensions running throughout black rhetorical traditions. After establishing in the first chapter the case for the DJ as digital griot and the digital griot as a model for multimedia writing instruction and for a new conception of the scholar activist working to build community, I use the ubiquitous practices of mix, remix, and mixtape as tropes for examining various texts and spaces to weave together oral, print, and digital manifestations of African American rhetoric in order to examine problems and possibilities, practices and processes, with technologies and digital writing firmly grounded in black rhetorical traditions, both for the benefit of black students and scholars and for all students and the entire discipline.

Chapter 2 begins with the rhetorical practice of the mix in order to think about the complex layerings that have redefined—for me at least—what it means to do intellectual work and what it means to teach composition, not only in the university but in community spaces as well. Chapter 3 considers the remix not only as revision but as central to African American collective memory in the everyday storytelling genre of the "back in the day" narrative. Chapter 4 presents Black Theology as a "mixtape movement," as the only movement in the history of the African American freedom struggle built explicitly as an intentional synthesis of the radical democratic (integrationist) and nationalist traditions in that struggle. The final chapter offers a reflection on what the work of building an African American rhetoric 2.0 that blends traditions and futures might look like. Finally, similar to the DJ's bringing together of a community of listeners and texts through the roll call and shoutout, I intersperse brief shoutouts to various digital griot projects created by people throughout the country to at least briefly point to the many possibilities that exist for people interested in this model.

cut break mix scratch bootleg remix layer mixtape loop fade call and response signifyin pastiche move the crowd enter the conversation change the game own your own take them *there*.

1

Groove: Synchronizing African American Rhetoric and Multimedia Writing through the Digital Griot

> It is important that people understand the roles and power that the griot has been endowed with since the beginning. One of the roles that the griot in African society had before the Europeans came was maintaining a cultural and historical past with that of the present.
>
> —D'Jimo Kouyate, "The Role of the Griot"

> If, in Ellison, history appears in the form of a groove, then the mixing tactics of DuBois and DJs provide ways to noisily bring together competing and complementary beats without sublimating their tensions.
>
> —Alexander G. Weheliye, Phonographies: Sonic Grooves in Afro-Modernity

AS COMPOSITION THEORY AND TEACHING undergo a repositioning that values cultural diversity and interrogates more deeply the social contexts in which writing occurs and as they place more importance on multiliteracies and multimedia writing, certain questions persist: What relationships exist between digital communication and other forms, other genres, other traditions? How do we understand the connections that will endure between text and screen, between image and voice, between the oral and the textual? In the case of African Americans and other people of color working for more equal access to technologies, the challenge to connect histories of technology with cultural histories becomes even more pressing. That challenge, as Bruce Sinclair argues in *Technology and the African-American*

Experience: Needs and Opportunities for Study, is to "bring together two subjects strongly connected but long segregated from each other" (1). Strengthening these connections demands much historical work, Sinclair notes, not only to develop solid understandings about the ways cultures and technologies—and race and technology—are intertwined but also to influence the production, consumption, and uses of technology in the present: asking "how race and technology reconstruct each other in radio and other media" can lead to greater participation and even structural change, though such change does not emerge as a given from such knowledge (11).

That composition and African American rhetoric are in a new age and in need of the same integration work Sinclair calls for is beyond doubt. Despite the major gaps that exist in cross-talk between work in multimedia writing and African American rhetoric and other American ethnic rhetorics, there is also good news in that even in the midst of these silences, there is much room for the links, connections, and overlap between these multiple areas that can make synchronizing them possible as well as a few key works that point the way to a more thorough remix, re-vision, of our disciplinary narrative. Scholarship in computers and writing is now nearly three decades old, and even scholars once perceived as Aristotelians focused exclusively on print like Andrea Lunsford are making the case for multimedia writing as central to how we reimagine composition as a field. In her 2005 Computers and Writing Conference keynote address, she argues that digital writing and our immersion in multiple media forms and spaces demands a return to performance as an important area in writing instruction:

> Crescendoing in the last two decades, the arts and crafts associated with the fifth canon have moved to the center of our discipline. To view writing as an active performance—that is as an act always involving the body and performance—enriches I. A. Richards' notion of the "interanimation of words": it is not only that individual words shift meaning given their context within a sentence, but also that words shift meaning given their embodied context and their physical location in the world. (170)

Our immersion in so many media and technologies becomes a central element of what writing has become, with Lunsford calling for a "secondary literacy . . . both highly inflected by oral forms, structures and rhythms and highly aware of itself as writing understood as variously organized and mediated systems of communication" (170).

Annette Harris Powell's study of a technology camp she and others developed for middle school students helps us understand the work we have left to do in equalizing access and challenges us to rethink exactly what we mean by access; her rethinking of access leads us to understand that everyday performances, rhetorical practices, and acts of writing lie at its (grass)roots. Borrowing from James Paul Gee's and Deborah Brandt's understanding of literacy as social practice and Pierre Bordieu's notion of habitus, she challenges us to understand access not as a thing to be acquired or achieved but as a complex "practice," a continual process of being socialized into the attitudes, behaviors, and engagements of a communicative space. By pulling back from individual examples of technologies to be used or learned and engaging a broader network of cultural practices, her study provides a context within and against which the situated technology and discursive practices of individuals and collectives, like some of the students in her project, can be read. It also points the way to some of the Afrofuturistic synchronizing that our discipline needs by explicitly linking black rhetorical practices to both multicultural writing instruction and technology in ways very similar to Lunsford's call for us to reinsert the fifth canon into writing instruction. Oral, print, and digital work become woven in much the same way that Columbus (Ted) Grace linked oral and print literacy instruction.

Perhaps the most powerful example yet in our extant literature of this synchronizing—of the ways that black rhetorical traditions can form crucial links between oral, print, and digital communication and digitized, rhetoricized conceptions of access for African American users and for everyone—is Carmen Kynard's work documenting black students' use of Blackboard in her writing classes. In this study, she shows how one of the core tropes and rhetorical practices of the African American oral tradition, signifyin, was a definitive feature of her students' writing practices on Bb. In fact, their heavy use of signifyin, or what she identifies as "Blackboard Flava Flavin" (heavy signifyin on scholarly texts, writing assignments, peers' Bb entries, the instructor, and themselves), becomes a crucial element of her students' process of claiming agency as writers in digital spaces. This ability to link technology use and practice to their own traditions helps the students claim a powerful rhetorical agency that is both critical and functional, allowing them to therefore become what Kynard calls "Afrodigitized."

Kynard's study shows us the foolishness of trying to scratch or sample the practices of the DJ, MC, or hype-wo/man in Hip Hop and drop them into our scholarship without thorough, searching attention to the discursive and rhetorical traditions from which they emerge. Such isolated sampling or ripping has some explanatory power, as Jeff Rice argues persuasively in his book *Rhetoric of Cool* (and before that in the influential *CCC* article "The 1963 Hip Hop Machine") and as work from people like Stuart Selber, Johndan Johnson-Eilola, and Geoffrey Sirc attests, but it also risks becoming yet another in the long line of those who have "taken our blues and gone," as Langston Hughes would call it, if we somehow build our theorizing on individual practices without full recognition of the people, networks, and traditions that have made these practices their gift to the broader culture. The recent video game *DJ Hero* and its appropriation of the DJ provide the perfect example of the danger of such isolated ripping. The game reduces the practices of the DJ to a mere cross-fader and turntable. While I'm not one to have a problem with a creative video game, I'm interested in far more than simply the isolated techniques of scratching on a turntable or hitting a cross-fader—for me, it is the wide range of cultural practices, multiple literacies, rhetorical mastery, and knowledge of traditions that DJs in black traditions represent that make them griots, link them to other griotic figures, and offer a model for writing that thoroughly weaves together oral performance, print literacy, mastery and interrogation of technologies, and technologies that can lead to a renewed vision for both composition and African American rhetoric. In *Digital Griots*, I attempt to bring those blues back, bring that beat back, so we can build theories, pedagogies, and practices

of multimedia writing that honor the traditions and thus the people
who are still too often not present in our classrooms, on our facul-
ties, in our scholarship.

By linking the DJ to other griotic figures and the broader network of rhetorical practices and traditions from which these figures
emerge, I want to ask a broader question. Instead of focusing exclusively on the writing practices of students or the practices we want
them to develop or the rhetorical practices that take place in a remix
culture, I'm interested in the rhetorical possibilities that emerge
from the culture that gave us the remix. The preacher, storyteller,
standup comic, everyday black people in conversation, and the DJ
can help black students see themselves reflected more genuinely in
writing classrooms and theory and can benefit all students looking
for a greater appreciation of the multiple connected and diverging
cultural influences on writing in a society that is (very slowly) becoming more genuinely inclusive and multicultural.

Because technology use, production, and design (and the role
each plays in the public imagination) are all so thoroughly embed-
ded in rhetorical acts, one could argue that technologies themselves
are rhetorical in nature. This rhetorical nature extends from the first
imaginings that lead to invention and design to decisions about
which designs to pursue; marketing to convince users that particular designs will be beneficial; the writing of content; the design of
interfaces; the social and cultural understandings that lead people to
adopt or avoid particular artifacts and processes; the writing of and
debates about policies governing technology use, design, production,
and marketing; budgetary decisions in governments, schools, businesses, and homes; instruction to develop skills and make a software
package or tool or piece of hardware relevant to users—all of these
rhetorical acts and more shape our relationships with technologies.
An important place to start to examine the ways African American
culture and technologies are intertwined, therefore, is with African
American rhetorical practices and traditions. In this book, I hope
to build on the growing calls from scholars in several disciplines
for more depth and range of study at the intersections of race and
technology by asking two related questions: How can sustained

inquiry into African American rhetoric help to develop models of meaningful, engaged technology access and use? And how can such models contribute to culturally relevant, culturally responsible instruction for all students, and especially African American students, when the rapid shifts in technologies result in exponentially greater expectations of teachers of writing at all levels?

It is my contention that any answer to those two questions must thoroughly weave together print, oral, and digital traditions and must offer models of black discursive and rhetorical excellence in order to move both public discourse and scholarly conversations beyond the continuous loops of polarizing Ebonics debates that are often rooted in scorn for the very students we want to serve and assumptions that black students can't do or won't do. In fact, let me just say this now for the record: at this moment in 2011, anyone still attempting to argue that Ebonics is a problem for black students or that it is somehow connected to a lack of intelligence or lack of desire to achieve is about as useful as a Betamax video cassette player, and it's time for those folks to be retired, be they teachers, administrators, or community leaders, so the rest of us can try to do some real work in the service of equal access for black students and all students. The linguistic case is settled, the scholarly case is clear, and there is too much pedagogical and practical work out there demonstrating the richness, beauty, and rhetorical power to be found in Ebonics for anyone to still be tryin to dismiss black students' abilities based on these (sometimes intentionally) ignorant positions. The griot helps move us beyond these tired debates and toward a model of rhetorical excellence rooted in black language use.

In her search for an archetype for engaging questions about African American relationships to technologies that moved beyond the utopian/dystopian polemic present in many technology narratives, Alondra Nelson based her concept of Afrofuturism on the necromancy of Ishmael Reed's HooDoo protagonist Papa LaBas and his combination of futuristic vision and commitment to grounding that vision in a deep, searching knowledge of the past. This combination and the committed, constant search that undergirds it helps to create conditions where the next generation will be successful in creating a text that can codify Black culture: past, present, and future. Rather than a "Western" image of the future that is increasingly detached from the past, or equally problematic, a future-primitive perspective that fantasizes an uncomplicated return to ancient culture, LaBas foresees the distillation of African diasporic experience, rooted in the past but not weighed down by it, contiguous yet continually transformed. (8)

Reed's use of LaBas as protagonist and Nelson's adoption of LaBas as a kind of ultimate protagonist and model for blackfolk in the United States and worldwide engaging technology issues is fascinating because of LaBas's role in the oral tradition. Papa LaBas is also referred to as Papa Legba and is the ultimate linguist in the Afrodiasporic oral tradition from Yoruba culture in Nigeria to Brazil, Cuba, Haiti, and, thanks in large part to Reed's novels, the United States as well. Legba links the spirit world with the physical, material world as the gatekeeper to both and is often portrayed as speaking all languages. In many ways, LaBas, especially as Nelson interprets him as a model for linking technologies and black identity, is the ultimate DJ and griot: an archivist, a canon maker, time binder; someone with an encyclopedic knowledge of traditions, a searing and searching awareness of contemporary realities, and the beat-matching, text-blending abilities to synchronize traditions, present realities, and future visions in that future text.

In devising ways to connect ancient rivers to the oceans of new realities and to confront the tragic ironies of watching young people who love language and who exhibit amazing linguistic and discursive skill in vernacular spaces yet find themselves struggling inside an Achievement Gap discourse within the education system, the late Ted Grace, storyteller and educator, developed a method he termed Oral Narrative Engagement (ONE) to connect instruction in print literacies to black oral traditions in tales that affirmed his students and showed them that there was beauty in their language, such as in the Anansi and Brer Rabbit stories. The folktales offered Grace's students (1) continual practice with language, (2) a view of language as living and dynamic, which reflects the love black people worldwide have for it and show outside the academy, (3) the chance to come to voice in developing their own versions of stories, (4) a model of rhetorical excellence developed through an awareness of audience, (5) a commitment to craft in shaping one's own style and delivery, and most important, (6) a body of texts that reflects African American communal values to be honored and celebrated in school settings. Through the exploits and trials of tricksters like Brer Rabbit, the Signifyin Monkey, Shine, Stagolee, and others, students were able to see epistemologies and ontologies that prized the wide range of ideological stances between the maintenance of healthy black communities, participation in the larger society, and resistance to domination and exclusion.

Both Nelson, in her exploration of black relationships to technologies in a digital age, and Grace, in his search for more effective, more inclusive literacy pedagogy for black students, turn to the storytelling tradition as a central component in the search. The importance of the story, of narrative in African American rhetorical traditions, to efforts at both participation in American society and resistance to oppression, to documenting the horrors and celebrating the joys, makes the griots the figures who are entrusted to tell the story and, through the practices they employ in recording, preserving, sharing, and even masking the knowledge of those stories, useful figures on which to base an African American rhetoric for a multimedia age that might ensure that new realities do not erase those "ancient rivers" that Langston Hughes reminds us connect young people to elders and ancestors and the Mississippi to the Euphrates, Nile, and Congo.

The black oral tradition that forms the basis, or the initial bridge, in Grace's model and Nelson's theoretical approach to engagements with technology, whether maintained in storytelling, sermons, song, poetry, standup comedy, or other forms, is so important to considerations of literacy for many reasons. Musicologist Joel Dinerstein, in his study of jazz, *Swinging the Machine: Modernity, Technology, and African American Culture between the World Wars*, develops Albert Murray's phrase "survival technology" by defining it this way: "Survival technology consists of public rituals of music, dance, storytelling, and sermonizing that create a forum for existential affirmation through physicality, spirituality, joy, and sexuality—'somebodiness'—as some African American preachers call it—against the dominant society's attempts to eviscerate one's individuality and cultural heritage" (22). In expanding his readers' ways of viewing technology, he makes the argument that during the industrial age, European Americans "created the nation's technology while African Americans created the nation's *survival technology*" (22). Examples of this "survival technology" and some of the links in this tradition are in order here. While John Henry is often the folktale most cited as an example of what Dinerstein and Alexander G. Weheliye call the black techno-dialogic at work in its folk tradition, it seems to me that "Shine and the Titanic" (along with John Jasper's classic sermon "De Sun Do Move") best illustrates the richness of black engagements with technology, from reflections on what it means to be human in relationship to technologies to critique and resistance and the ways those engagements are woven thoroughly into the griotic tradition from past centuries to the present. Both texts, and especially the Shine tale, highlight African American skepticism of white, Western reverence—even worship—of technology and the fierce determination that black people have always had to be free, to assert their own individual and collective humanity in relationship with technologies and in resistance to systems of domination. The Shine narrative lives to this day in the name of a Hip Hop MC and in the same Steve Harvey (in *The Original Kings of Comedy*) performance I cite in chapter 3. Shine, a derogatory term for black people throughout the early twentieth century, becomes the name of a laborer on the *Titanic*, the ship everyone knows by now was symbolic of Western technological innovation, expertise, and domination. As a laborer—and the only black person on the ship—Shine participated in that technological system and its assumptions, if you will, in order to have a job but also knew when it was time to be out, when it was time to challenge those assumptions. When the ship started to sink, Shine jumped overboard and decided to make his own way home, preferring to duel with sharks than with white supremacy. In the kind of flipping of the script of power relations that often happens in the folktale tradition, bankers, captains of industry, and women offer all the money and loving he can imagine while begging Shine to help them out of the liquid jam that the ship's sinking was quickly becoming. But the refrain says it all: and Shine swam on. Whether sharks were at his heels or people were pleading with him to rescue them, Shine swam on. Despite every request, despite every challenge, despite every offer, Shine swam on. By the time it took the information networks of the day to transmit the news that the ship had sunk, Shine "was in Harlem on 125th Street, damn near drunk," home, among his people, living his life, having survived because he had the psychological armor that the tradition, wisely read and applied, offers and that Kamau Daáood tells his people we all need. In some ways, the refrain tells the real story, even more than the punchline of his successful return to Harlem: and Shine swam on. Its persistent repetition throughout the tale tells of dogged determination, confidence in his choice.

Black folktales receive significant scholarly attention as a central component of black culture, even through today, although those tales are not often read as examples of a black techno-dialogic tradition. The storyteller and preacher are oft-studied griotic figures in African American culture. The DJ as a griotic figure has received much less attention. The DJ has taken up many of these roles and has been grounded in many of these oral and folklore traditions for decades, sometimes completely under the radar. Before the separation of the DJ and the MC that marked the coming of age of mainstream success for Hip Hop, the DJ began as someone far more rooted in the oral tradition than he or she appears to be now. Early DJs (and many current ones) often announced records and artists in slick raps on the radio, creating personae rooted in characters like Shine and Stagolee, speaking in code to tell listeners details about mass meetings in the civil rights movement and initiating call and response chants in parties. While DJs have always been important rhetorical figures and have always been grounded in black oral traditions, their technological mastery and innovation have been just as significant to African American culture, opening doors to opportunity in past eras and ushering in an art form in Hip Hop that transformed American music and our notions of how narrative works in the process.

The technical proficiency of the DJ in Hip Hop has begun to attract the attention of some compositionists who value the ways Hip Hop has disrupted the notion of a linear text and the ways the art form has placed a focus on the recycling, reuse, and repurposing of language and tools old and new. In an attempt to escape the closed feedback loop guaranteed by a focus on the individual author working alone to create some kind of original product, and possibly in a beatnik kind of gesture toward resisting oppressive structures, policies, and practices, compositionists have settled on some of the practices of the DJ in the search for conceptual metaphors for the new work we must imagine and do. In this search, references to practices like the sample, mix, remix, and bootleg have become common in our disciplinary language. Despite this recent scholarly attention, the brilliance of the African American DJ is still often a thoroughly unappreciated phenomenon and, when noticed, is often noticed in ways that completely remove that brilliance from the cultural traditions and histories that led to the emergence of the DJ as a rhetorical figure every bit as important as the preachers, teachers, poets, and political activists we usually study within rhetoric. Selber, Johnson-Eilola, Rice, Sirc, and others in the discipline have attended carefully to the practices of the DJ as offering potential to help us rethink writing instruction. Johnson-Eilola and Selber, in a *Computers and Composition* article, "Plagiarism, Originality, Assemblage," build significantly on Rebecca Moore Howard's longstanding calls for new approaches to punitive plagiarism policies and outdated notions of authorial originality and have also extended their discussion of the compositional practices of the DJ by asserting that we live and write in a remix culture. Their assertion, made through references to DJ Danger Mouse, Jay Z's *The Black Album*, and DJ Spooky, compels us to move beyond merely acknowledging or respecting the remix as rhetorical practice. Johnson-Eilola and Selber want us to consider new writing practices like pastiche, boilerplate, and assemblage as "equally valued" practices as the standard essay for the writing classroom (384). Further, they look to the remix to push further on conversations launched by James Porter and others calling for greater latitude for teachers and students in determining "fair use" of copyrighted materials.

Alex Reid and Daniel Anderson invoke music and what might be considered part of the progeny of the DJ's party set—the playlist—in order to inform both institutional practices and pedagogical practice. Reid documents the State University of New York at Cortland's implementation of iTunes University as a platform for delivering course content. He argues that technology convergence (the convergence of many different functions onto one tool like the iPhone or other smart phones and the convergence of media strategies and networks—individual companies delivering content across film, TV, YouTube, books, and radio, for example) and social networking among technology users creates a sea change in the writing practices of our students that we *must* respond to: "The ability to compose media and contribute it to a mobile network that includes a constellation of participatory sites indicates a permanent shift in the compositional practices and rhetorical relationships that have structured higher education to this point" ("Portable Composition" 66).

Teachers and scholars are hampered in their attempts to respond to these shifts, however, because of the necessarily slow bureaucratic processes of institutional curricular design and implementation—processes that are in place to ensure a needed critical, evaluative perspective instead of a whimsical response to whatever the need of the day might seem to be. Despite the challenges institutional structures might place in the way of teachers, however, "the contradictory, overlapping, open, closed, and fluctuating systems of exchanges that networks create" and in which our students participate in their everyday lives pose an even more important challenge to our thoughts about disciplinary identity and our individual identities as teachers and scholars. Reid cosigns Johnson-Eilola and Selber's call for a rethinking of authorship and an embrace of practices like assemblage, but he pushes further to argue that if we want to understand student writing practices and processes, we have to move beyond the student as individual writer and into a cultural understanding of the networks they inhabit (and in which they do the great majority of their writing). This call, of course, is very similar to that made by Cynthia Selfe and Gail Hawisher in their search to understand the "cultural ecologies" of technology literacy.

Anderson uses the playlist and collage to a different end—one of considering student motivation and building bridges between familiar literacies and those prized in the classroom, a tech-inflected version of Grace's linking of oral traditions and print literacy. His essay "The Low Bridge to High Benefits: Entry Level Multimedia, Literacies, and Motivation" also calls for a focus on the networks in which students live, play, work, and write, and he echoes Powell's understanding of access and literacy as activities and processes rather than things. He hopes to use familiar, even fun activities like writing with video, collage, playlists, and video games in order to develop "critiques as they look at design cultures . . . [and] use contexts, institutional forces, and popular representations of technology" (46), a goal similar to Stephanie Vie's in her article "Digital Divide 2.0: 'Generation M' and Online Social Networking Sites in the Composition Classroom." Anderson goes so far as to say that thinking of student motivation and connecting with the genres and practices they use in their everyday lives might lead us to teaching that could even "hold the potential for delivering body and soul realizations, engagement, educational magic" (46).

Aside from rich verbal play on the microphone, aside from the "remix," what makes the DJ worth more than a mention regarding the practices compositionists reference and sample? What makes this figure a griot? Many people are familiar with the figure of the griot, the storyteller found in many West African cultures. There is far more to the griot than storytelling, however, and this figure is alive on this side of the Atlantic in various forms. The griot is often a master of both words and music who is a storyteller, praise singer, and historian in many of those West African cultures. The griot is sometimes an entertainer, sometimes a counselor to chiefs and leaders, but regardless of the range between playful and serious, the griot is absolutely central to the life of his or her society, according to D'Jimo Kouyate. Beverly Robinson notes the importance of the trust the audience or community places in the griot, seeing his or her craft as "instrumental in holding a community of people of African heritage together when so many opposing elements challenged their physical, spiritual, and intellectual survival" (216). For Ivan Van Sertima, the role of folktales in African American culture, and especially the central figure of the trickster, is revolutionary—and not only in the sense of the powerful "longing of a powerless group, class, or race for social or political change, for transcendence over an oppressive order of relationships":

> I speak also of the revolutionary role of the trickster in a more radical and complex sense, a role Trickster played among aboriginal Africans and Americans, a role related to the profound and often obscure longing of the human psyche for freedom from fixed ways of seeing, feeling, thinking, acting; a revolt against a whole complex of "givens" coded into a society, a revolt which may affect not only an oppressed group, class, or race, but a whole order—the settled institutions and repetitive rituals of a whole civilization. (103)

Tom Hale, in his book *Griots and Griottes*, suggests that the role is even more than a combination of these elements and calls the griot a "time binder." Binding time, linking past, present, and future, the griot is keeper of history, master of its oral tradition, and rhetor extraordinaire, able to produce or perform on demand for whatever segment of the tribe requires it and whatever the situation demands—celebration, critique, preservation, connection. The griot and the tradition of stories that makes up the griot's craft reflect both participation in and resistance to the larger order and link past, present, and future, even in the midst of physical and psychic dislocation.

Both Paul D. Miller and Gilbert Williams, coming from very different places in examining the role of the DJ—Miller in the tradition of "turntablism" and Williams focused on the DJ as radio personality—make the case for the DJ as a griot. In Miller's book *Rhythm Science*, he identifies the DJ as storyteller and keeper of the culture. The DJ's craft, rhythm science, "uses an endless recontextualizing as a core compositional strategy" (21), and Miller notes that "the best DJs are griots, and whether their stories are conscious or unconscious, narratives are implicit in the sampling idea" (21). In other words, DJs are not mere ventriloquists, playing or telling other people's stories for us; rather, their arranging, layering, sampling, and remixing are inventions too, keeping the culture, telling their stories and ours, binding time as they move the crowd and create and maintain community. Williams, on the other hand, uses his book to make explicit the linguistic connection between the DJ and past griots, identifying them as crucial keepers of African American folk and oral traditions: through their rich verbal play used in every possible function, from introducing songs to selling products, promoting events, and even preaching sermons to rapping, rhyming, and signifyin, they "promote ideas and values their communities need to hear. As griots or storytellers they help shape the moral character of their listeners . . . as ministers, teachers, and jesters, they have become cultural heroes" (ix, x). From early DJs like Jack Cooper and Al Benson to Jazzy Joyce on the radio and Beth Coleman and DJ Spooky as turntablists and lecturers, oral traditions, print literacies, and technological mastery have been linked to make the griot truly a digital figure.

In linking traditional griotic figures like the preacher and storyteller with the more contemporary example of the DJ, positing the digital griot as a model for multimedia writing calls for a focus on the interconnectedness of print, oral, and digital media, a thorough knowledge of and grounding in African American discursive and rhetorical practices, and an ethos of commitment to community, in all of the rich ways writers might understand that term. The DJ, from the beginnings of black radio through Hip Hop and to the present, may be the most powerful example of how all of these qualities emerge in one figure's rhetorical practices. Long before Chuck D made his declaration that Hip Hop was black people's CNN, the black radio DJ fulfilled the griotic function of delivering and interpreting the news for African Americans. William Barlow's *Voice Over* and Timothy Tyson's *Radio Free Dixie* both attest to how radio was a central space for African American storytelling, identity formation, and community building. One might even argue that black radio was the home of an African American public sphere, a semipublic and a counterpublic space of engagement with and resistance to mainstream narratives, policies, and actions. Before 2007's movie *Talk to Me* about D.C. griot, poet, and isht talker extraordinaire Petey Greene, Spike Lee's warm, loving, and layered fictional portrayal in 1989's *Do the Right Thing* of Mister Señor Love Daddy, record spinner at W-E-L-O-V-E FM, stands as both celebration and lament of the centrality of the griotic black radio DJ and his or her demise at the hands of increasing corporate control of local radio stations and programming. Even before the Digital Millennium Copyright Act (DMCA) eviscerated the powerful communal role of the local radio DJ that Barlow documents in his study, Lee clearly positions Love Daddy as a central community figure, even the moral voice of the film. He comments on and interprets the actions of the film through his own words and the soundtrack he spins, knows all the characters and their individual stories, and bears the larger communal history. The omnipresence of radio (Radio Raheem!) and this station in everyone's lives throughout the film's Brooklyn neighborhood continually underscore this positioning. In his care to leave no rhetorical stone unturned, Lee literally and explicitly makes Love Daddy the bearer of communal truth—"that's the *triple* truth, Ruth!" Love Daddy tells the stories, carries the history, interprets the news, mediates the disputes, and helps shape the community's collective identity.

The griot has survived the middle passage, slavery, and centuries of American apartheid and has been diffused into many different spaces and figures: storytellers, preachers, poets, standup comics, DJs, and even everyday people all carry elements of the griot's role in African American culture. As historians and archivists, they interpret current events, raise societal critique, entertain, and pass down communal values. The spirit of the griot survives in all of these figures and in the centrality of oral traditions to African American communities, even as the nation as a whole has moved into a print-based and then a digital, multimedia culture. The "digital griot," an amalgamation of all of these figures, offers a useful model for conceptualizing black rhetorical excellence bridging print, oral, and digital communication, demonstrating

- knowledge of the traditions and cultures of his or her community (is grounded deeply in those traditions, and can "tell it");
- the technological skills and abilities to produce in multiple modalities;
- the ability to employ those skills for the purposes of building community and/or serving communities with which he or she is aligned;
- awareness of the layered ethical commitments and questions involved in serving any community;
- the ability to "move the crowd"—that is, use those traditions and practices and technologies for the purposes of persuasion.

On perhaps their most basic level, the practices of the DJ offer us important conceptual metaphors for writing practices we already teach and value:

- the shoutout as the use of references, calling the roll, and identifying and declaring one's relationships, allegiances, and influences as tools for building community and locating oneself in it
- crate-digging as continual research—not merely for the songs, hooks, breakbeats, riffs, texts, arguments, and quotes for a particular set or paper but as a crucial part of one's long-term work, of learning, knowing, and interpreting a tradition
- mixing as the art of the transition and as revision in the Adrienne Rich sense of writing as re-vision
- remix as critical interpretation of a text, repurposing it for a different rhetorical situation as 2010 Conference on College Composition and Communication chair Gwen Pough challenges the field to "remix: revisit, rethink, revise, renew" in the conference call
- mixtape as anthology, as everyday act of canon formation, interpretation, and reinterpretation
- sample as those quotes, those texts, those ideas used enough, important enough to our conceptions of what we are doing in a text (or even in our lifelong work) to be looped and continually repeated rather than merely quoted or referenced

More than these specific practices and abilities, however, the larger implications of the rhetorical practices in my sampled list above is the kind of theoretical orientation that not only can thoroughly weave together oral traditions, print literacies, and digital writing but can do so in the pursuit of both access and transformation, to give writers the tools for both participation in society and for revolt against the codes, or the complex of givens in a society, as Van Sertima notes above. Through these practices we can indeed answer Tricia Rose's challenge to "imagine these Hip Hop principles as a blueprint for social resistance and affirmation: create sustaining narratives, accumulate them, layer, embellish, and transform them" (*Black Noise* 39) and through this affirmation and transformation develop an approach to African American rhetorical study and to composition theory and practice that no longer consigns black students, writers, or scholars to token, "colored day at the carnival" status nor consigns digital theory, rhetoric, and writing as white by default because those areas and our American technology sector still appear to be so homogeneous. My argument in this book is that African Americans should take this griotic tradition to their engagements with technology, becoming digital griots, bearers of this tradition in digital spaces. I also suggest that the digital griot has much to offer teacher-scholars in literacy and composition looking for relevant models of multimodal literacies for their work and that of their students.

What are the skills, abilities, and understandings that this culture bearer brings to his or her work that can form the basis of multimodal writing? The wide range of genres and spaces of production for the DJ begins to answer this question: the on-air radio show; the mixtape; the sample; the bootleg; the flyers and posters used to promote artists, parties, and events; the studio session as producer for singers and MCs; the MC himself or herself as host and controller of the event or party. What skills and abilities allow the DJ to perform all of these roles and produce "texts" in all of these spaces? First, and perhaps most important, the DJ—especially a good or great one—knows an entire tradition of music and is a historiographer and up-to-the-minute improviser at the same time. He or she can tell you what was made when, who made it, who else was on the record, and what styles are present at different times. More than just knowing a tradition of music, however, the DJ can make seamless connections between the beats, styles, forms, harmonies, and ideas of various points in those traditions and the present. Second, the DJ must master a range of different techniques and technologies: layering, blending, sampling, mixing, collaging, altering elements like bass lines or melodies or vocals, as well as the ever-changing tools and technologies of the radio or production studio. More and more, the DJ must master these skills across many different platforms and tools—cutting edge, trailing edge, and everything in between. Third, the role of the DJ is richly rhetorical because playing records or reciting rhymes or mastering technologies alone is never enough. The DJ has to know his or her audience enough to know what to say and what to play at all times in real time: what to play to get people to stop standing on the walls and get out on the dance floor, to get them from just dancing and posing on the floor to really enjoying themselves, to break the ice between people who might be glancing at each other, to take the crowd "there" to that ecstatic place where even people who are not on the floor tap into memories, playing in the tensions between familiar associations and new connections, new contexts, and experience the kind of release that sends them home drenched in sweat and the sensory. The DJ creates and recreates community with every performance, be it in the club, in the studio, or on the radio, and thus must understand the commonplaces, must know and share in their experiences even when he or she takes on the role of challenging the crowd or community to go to new texts, new places. When the DJ takes on the role of producer, it is his or her job to place an artist's voice, style, and approach into conversation with others in a genre and/or to stake out new and innovative space for that artist. In the space of the radio show, the DJ also fulfills the role of interpreter for the community, reporting events, interviewing guests, and providing both context and worldview. These community connections demand the fourth element of that rhetorical, griotic role: in order to perform these

multiple acts of community-building, DJs must be intimately connected with their community, no matter what other communities
they might have access to.

Again, moving beyond skills and abilities, beyond specific practices to a broader sense of why the DJ is a digital griot, it is the DJ
who is the model of the kinds of synchronizing of traditions and
future texts and can allow for deeper, more meaningful links between black rhetorical traditions and technologies, between African
American rhetoric and multimedia writing. Through the cut, break,
sample, mix, remix, mixtape, and a continual, crate-digging search
through past, present, and future texts, the DJ maintains the groove
that allows narrative, text, and history to continue while allowing for
new voices, new arguments. Alexander Weheliye, in *Phonographies*,
examines the ways that black traditions have linked orality, writing,
and technology so that "instead of emphasizing either the technological or the cultural, the grooves of Afro-modernity integrate both"
(16). In articulating this twin focus and identifying the DJ as the
figure who helps us with this synchronizing, Weheliye argues that
without such synchronizing, none of us has a theoretical leg to stand
on: discourses of culture and technology "are neither erased nor
suspended; rather, they are significantly recreated in their encounter
with auditory Blackness, which also undergoes substantial shifts in
this assemblage. In this way, neither of these energies can materialize
without its spectral doppelganger: no western modernity without
(sonic) Blackness and no Blackness in the absence of modernity"
(45). Weheliye develops this point in more direct reference to the DJ
in the introduction to his book:

> One of the major currents of sonic Afro-modernity is "the
> mix" as it appears in Souls [W. E. B. Du Bois's Souls of Black
> Folk] and DJing, for it offers an aesthetic that realigns the tem-
> poralities (grooves) of Western modernity in its insistence on
> rupture and repetition. If, in [Ralph] Ellison, history appears
> in the form of a groove, then the mixing tactics of DuBois
> and DJs provide ways to noisily bring together competing and
> complementary beats without sublimating their tensions. (13)

Speaking of finding value in the "noise," Rose's classic *Black Noise* examines what the DJ offers rhetors and asks what the mix and remix give us:

> What is the significance of flow, layering, and rupture as demonstrated on the body and in Hip Hop's lyrical, music, and visual works? Interpreting these concepts theoretically, one can argue that they create and sustain rhythmic motion, continuity, and circularity via flow; accumulate, reinforce, and embellish this continuity through layering; and manage threats to these narratives by building in ruptures that highlight the continuity as it momentarily challenges it. These effects at the level of style and aesthetics suggest affirmative ways in which profound social dislocation and rupture can be managed and perhaps contested in the cultural arena. Let us imagine these Hip Hop principles as a blueprint for social resistance and affirmation: create sustaining narratives, accumulate them, layer, embellish, and transform them. However, be also prepared for rupture, find pleasure in it, in fact, *plan on* social rupture. When these ruptures occur, use them in creative ways that will prepare you for a future in which survival will demand a sudden shift in ground tactics. (39)

So, in theoretical terms, the combination of the DJ's practices with his or her mastery of cutting, leading, bleeding, and trailing edge technologies and constant searching of traditions in the attempt to create the future text helps us to imagine both social resistance and affirmation, helps us to link divergent and sometimes competing narratives without flattening their differences, and helps us to keep cultures and technologies linked. Beyond this general orientation toward technological engagement and textual creation, though, the DJ is also an ideal rhetorical model for multimedia writing. One reason why the DJ as a digital griot provides such a model is because this figure is an example of the intense commitment to craft that rhetorical excellence requires. Those people who become DJs are willing to spend the hundreds and thousands of hours it takes to become proficient in this craft because it is learned in a space where the learners' identities are not under constant threat or outright attack; instead, the space is one where their humanity and ability are taken for granted, even while the expectations of rhetorical excellence and agility are always high. Furthermore, there is room for a balance between individual identity and participation in broader communities; room for the voices, styles, and personae the learners actually want to develop even as they must learn to participate in many different discursive spaces. If learners spent the many required hours on the tables in the studio or bedroom or basement (Grandmaster Flash learned in his mother's kitchen, documented in the 1982 movie *Wild Style*), they can do it and still be who they want to be, without having to check their identity at the door as the cost of success.

One assumption present in my list of reasons for arguing that writers see themselves as digital griots is a focus on African American students writing for their own communities, as well as on all students writing for multiple communities. There are several reasons for inserting this assumption at the outset, a primary one being that of all the audiences composition classrooms imagine for their students, rarely is the home community included. Usually phrases like "academic discourse," "civic writing," or "professional writing" guide our theorizing and pedagogy, whether individually or in combination, all implying that the main—or even the only—goal is to prepare students to move away from the home community and its discursive practices. For African American students, this division can lead to two particular dangers. The first is the continued "miseducation of the Negro," the well-known phrase Carter G. Woodson used to identify the heightened alienation many African Americans felt from their communities the more education they pursued. The second danger is that instruction that disconnects students from their home communities and the discursive practices and traditions of those communities risks denying students powerful examples and sources of knowledge to be used in academic, civic, professional, and other kinds of discourse. Ted Grace, referenced above, studied black student performance in English/language arts classes when African American oral traditions were used as a basis for learning print-based literacies and found that this approach resulted in both greater student interest in a curriculum they saw as relevant and greater performance on print literacy standards in mainstream curricula. Geneva Smitherman found similar results in a different study: in her article "The Blacker the Berry, the Sweeter the Juice," she notes that African American students whose twelfth grade National Assessment of Educational Progress test essays demonstrated familiarity with black discursive patterns scored higher than students who weren't as familiar with such patterns, showing that students grow more in standardized English use and mainstream discourses when they are at home in their own language traditions.

The combination of Dinerstein's notion of the oral tradition and the concept of DJ as important bearer of black survival technology presents the wide range of African American humanity and knowledge present in the vernacular spaces of the culture, or as Daryl Cumber Dance notes in her collection of African American folklore, *From My People*, in the lives of everyday, "drylongso" blackfolk. The deeply ingrained stereotypes that still operate in much public discourse and mainstream media prevent many people from having any contact with or knowledge of the breadth of this range. Another reason African American oral traditions should be central in any kind of literacy instruction, and especially in multimodal literacy instruction, is that they provide a wealth of content reflecting black epistemologies and ontologies, ways of knowing and being in the world that begin with the assumption of black humanity, and provide examples of the wide continuum from access to, participation in, and resistance of broader narratives and structures. A third reason for a focus on the depth and complexity in African American oral traditions through the figure of the griot and forms like folktales, toasts, double-dutch rhymes, blues, Hip Hop, and more is that it can provide a familiar bridge to other forms of literacy that offer relevance and begin with the premise of black mastery and celebration of language, of work and play in language, of the individual performer's and the audience's or community's expectations, and of the importance of both skills and critical consciousness. Finally, an approach to literacy grounded in the figure of the griot and in oral traditions allows discussion of the discursive practices that take place in all communities from a descriptive perspective rather than a prescriptive one. Signifyin, call and response, woofin, toasting, masking, the blues, testifying, the shoutout, freestyle, and the battle rhyme—rather than merely scratching the polemic surface of linguistic disrespect that attends most public discourse and much teacher lore about Ebonics and African American students, these practices offer incredible fields to mine. The tradition links the experiences and histories of U.S. blacks with those in the Caribbean, South and Central America, Africa, and the rest of the diaspora. The figure of storyteller as griot in the black tradition also helps establish connections to storytelling traditions in all cultures. Exploration of the innovative practices and conceptual frameworks fostered by black DJs in the Hip Hop tradition opens up space for connection with everyone and every culture as well, as Hip Hop DJing has influenced the entire society—just as Robert Johnson and B. B. King influenced guitar playing through and beyond rock and other cultures and musical genres worldwide. Theory rooted in and celebrating black culture and its contributions while opening up space for intersectional analysis, intergenerational inquiry, intercultural connection—that's some of what the digital griot offers us: a new groove, mixed, remixed, and mixtaped to "noisily bring together competing and complementary beats without sublimating their tensions."

Shoutout: digNubia (www.dignubia.org)

This digital griot project, developed by Ronald Bailey, uses ancient Nubia as a site of inquiry to help young people connect the sciences and humanities. Through an interactive Web site, documentary films, workshops, traveling exhibitions, and resource materials created for parents and educators, digNubia uses archaeology as an interdisciplinary way to introduce students to science, technology, engineering, and mathematics. By connecting young people to black culture, digNubia works to "strengthen SMET [science, mathematics, engineering, technology] literacy in underserved communities by delivering materials and activities that meet the demands of national standards; to strengthen the capacity of community based educators and organizations to create additional opportunities for SMET education; and to spark an interest in young people in career opportunities in the sciences." The key here is that Bailey and his team link inquiry in science and technology to African American and African history and culture, helping young people see themselves in the story to "resonate with African American audiences and find new ways to reach young people in African American communities."

2

Mix: Roles, Relationships, and Rhetorical Strategies in Community Engagement

> My interest is not merely in the ways Black students can learn; I
> am also concerned about the psychic costs they pay. A pedagogy
> is only successful if it makes knowledge or skill achievable while
> at the same time allowing students to maintain their own sense
> of identity.
>
> —Keith Gilyard, Voices of the Self

AS FUNK ARTIST ROGER TROUTMAN declared in 1984, it's in the mix.
What? Music is in the mix; writing is in the mix. In the constantly
new and renewing possibilities that are emergent in the many complex practices of the DJ providing the mix: selection, arrangement,
layering, sampling, beat-matching, blending. In the thought that
anything—any sample, any sound, any tradition, any clip—is available to be used in any text. The idea that layering different voices
and grooves, mining all of a musical tradition, and hacking, jacking
loops, chords, melodies, riffs, and any kind of other sound from all
kinds of other musical traditions, is a valued musical—and writing—practice. It's in the idea that a writer's particular mix and
the view of music, language, and tradition it espouses might be as
important as a linear vocal or instrumental performance, that it *is*
the performance, that it is the point, the thesis, the argument. For
a scholar pursuing community work as an important part of his
or her overall scholarly agenda, it's all in the mix, too, rather than
in the power of any thesis I might spout or any argument I might
make. How does one come up with the right blend of intellectual

influences, the right balance of how to allocate one's time, an appropriate position within the multiple and competing discourses that frame a department's, university's, or discipline's expectations for one's work?

Finding this right mix is a difficult task because theoretical and practical models abound in our disciplinary conversation for many different approaches to community-based literacy work—for individual projects, for institutional relationships and agendas, and for undergraduate and graduate curricula. And it's difficult because there are so many other sources, so many other voices, so many other sounds inside and outside the academy, so many other echoes, loops, samples, and riffs to be explored. But how can or should the individual scholar imagine his or her role as one committed to community work? What models or approaches exist that might help one to navigate the many, and conflicting, audiences and expectations such a scholar is expected to—and wants to—serve? How does one build and maintain healthy relationships with communities that somehow do not replicate that miseducation of the Negro—either the miseducation of black communities and their members or of the scholar of any ethnicity who would hope to work with those communities? In this chapter, I argue that it is impossible to develop a successful model of scholarship that is genuinely community-based. Further, I argue that such a search for "success" in one's community work or for successful models is a fruitless task that should be avoided. Rather than searching for what works or will work or will be rewarded by university structures, or creating demonstrable or measurable success according to some matrix or set of desired outcomes or so-called best practices, or pursuing that one profound argument, that compelling statement that people want to adopt or debate, one should think about how he or she can create the best possible mix, or specific layering of the many different expectations and discourses that must be confronted, and the intellectual, theoretical, pedagogical, and political commitments he or she is willing to make. The digital griot offers one such approach for the mix of roles, relationships, and rhetorical practices the scholar might engage. The blend I present attempts to speak to the difficult terrain one chooses to tread when a scholar is fundamentally committed to social justice and societal transformation, works collaboratively with local communities, teaches in the idiom of the communities he or she seeks to serve, and uses technologies toward the ends of building and serving community. After exploring the role the griot might play in guiding one's approach to community work, I present some of the story of how I have tried to build on this approach and then offer an outline of a community course based on the digital griot—a course that presents my take on the theoretical and pedagogical mixes that are necessary to teach writing and to teach African American rhetoric in a multimedia age.

In spite of the multiple practices that are all referred to as mixing in the DJ's craft, the rhetorical work of the mix as I mean it in this chapter extends in two directions. The first is in the production or the creation of an individual track or text; the second has to do with the way a DJ is able to line up two different tracks so that they connect seamlessly. In the first case, the DJ is adding, arranging, and layering components in a single song. Chicago-based MC Common and his DJ, aptly named "Mr. DJ" (cuing up a 1990s song by R/B group Zhane), talk about the wide range of elements far beyond the beats and rhymes each considers when putting together a track. Common often does as many as twenty takes per track to achieve not only the kind of delivery he wants but the ways he wants those various elements arranged. "I like the mids and the highs pushed," he says. "I want that crispness in my voice. Without knowing technically how it works, I always look for that sizzle" (qtd. in Micaller 23–24). Mr. DJ, on the other hand, is always considering the technical and technological demands involved in getting Common the sound he wants. He frequently completes basic outlines of tracks with some live elements before Common comes in, but "it's just a skeleton so he can hear the melodies. I do the bulk of the live instruments post-vocal so I can add sounds that accentuate the vocal and the words" (24). Those elements might come from anywhere in a collection of over six thousand albums—hi-hat from one place, snares from another, bass line from somewhere else, using software like Reason, Logic, ProTools, all of this in addition to sometimes bringing in live instrumentalists to play an exact line that he has already programmed. Questlove, drummer and audiophile from The Roots, describes his attentiveness to the incessant layering in one of his favorite Public Enemy songs, "It Takes a Nation of Millions," in an interview with Dale Coachman in *Waxpoetics*. Asked by Coachman what he listened for in the production of the song, Questlove responded:

> Every time I heard it, I heard something new. First, I had to hear it to clear all the samples in my head. Sony Walkmans were so innovative you could just pull the jack halfway out and start hearing other things, like these stereoized samples and the subliminal stuff. Then it finally hit me—this is my father's record collection! I go home and verify all the breaks from my father's collection and then it's like "now I know what my calling is." (34)

Questlove's intervention into the musical text by pulling the jack partially out of the Walkman in order to hear more and different sounds recalls Alex Weheliye's introduction to *Phonographies* in which he uses the apparition as metaphor to explain the ways a compelling passage calls, even requires, the listener to use the available technologies to intervene in the text. The listener becomes a literal ghost chaser in order to bring that beat back, to hear that section again. Questlove also hints at the griot's role as archivist, with his drive to chase down every sample and clear it in his head, no matter how esoteric. Ean Golden, in a column designed to teach newbies some of the tricks of the trade, discusses some of the rhetorical value of the mix—the need for someone on the wheels to be able to make the right transitions in both tempo and feel: "Maintaining the musical pace and feel in a mix is a very important facet of DJing. . . . All forms of music have an ingrained pattern of rhythm, tension and release that we all naturally expect to hear. When those patterns are broken in a mix, it can throw off the dancers and the vibe in general" (48).

I almost never heard my father's record collection, literally or figuratively, in connection to my work as an academic or a compositionist—until I got to Penn State, that is. And even after having heard that collection and my mentor's intellectual, theoretical, and literal record collections in my graduate work, I still didn't quite hear my own blend yet, my own mix. I didn't hear it in the many layers of the individual track of my intellectual commitments, nor did I envision it yet in the mix between the many different tracks of an academic career (check chapter 4)—especially when I considered the blend between the campus and disciplinary role of the scholar and the attempt to employ my work in some kind of service, some kind of community engagement.

I've always resisted the challenge to write about community work, until now. Not because I didn't have models—I had powerful examples of intellectual guides layering those elements and blending those tracks in Keith Gilyard and Elaine Richardson. And not because I didn't have some clarity around the elements themselves: what I cared about, what my abilities were, what the needs were inside the classroom, discipline, academy, and community. I had my ideas. I just didn't quite have that mix I needed within and between the tracks. I suppose this is why I never wanted to write about my own work, or in broader terms to/with/about the conversations taking place in our field about community literacy or community engagement. In fact, I often resist the task of writing grant requests, though secure funding clearly would make much of the work I attempt to do a great deal easier. Several of my colleagues have challenged me on these issues. For example, in our many hallway and office and pre- or post-meeting conversations at Syracuse, Steve Parks has reminded me that leveraging funds that can directly affect communities is important work. He has persuaded me that, for a scholar having any pretense toward caring about the communities with which he or she works, that person must develop sustainable projects that have a chance to live beyond the fly-by-night ideas many of us have. Of course, however, as I have always told Steve and many more friends and colleagues, staying away from grants means remaining free to pursue my own vision, play with, revise, reject, start over, however I and those I collaborate with see fit. In some ways, though, he reminds me, as does Jeff Grabill in his influential book *Community Literacy Programs and the Politics of Change*, that confronting the slow, deliberative pace of universities and other public institutions and the straitjacketing language of grant applications and laws and policies must be a part of community work, no matter how idealistic one might be or no matter how much I might yearn for the intellectual freedom to do what I want to do. And Steve is a good example of a scholar bringing informed political commitment to bear on universities and funding institutions in pursuit of using literacy in the struggle for fundamental changes in our society for working people. Still I resist. Try as I might, I can't pretend that I have answers that others in our field who have written on the subject have, even when I've been convinced that some of those answers from some of those scholars were arrived at in far too facile a way or in ways that seemed to take advantage of their subjects in order to claim some grand commitment to "the community" that I was sure never really existed. So even if some scholars have seemed to pimp their service for some scholarly-career-social-security (and I'm not saying that there is anyone who seems that way to me now, simply that there was a time when I read work in community literacy far less attentively and far more dismissively), I could not and cannot honestly blame my resistance on such a phenomenon. The "they don't *really* care about the folk" argument just doesn't work, because I've witnessed far too many creative projects and scholars who write about such work with passion and commitment and clarity. Yet my resistance remains, even as I work on this chapter.

There are many reasons for my resistance to writing on this subject: I don't like having to describe this kind of work in the language of grant funders or other scholars; I absolutely detest the thought of having to describe a project as if it has produced specific quantifiable or documentable results. In fact, I often feel ill at ease even talking about community work. I don't think I'm good at it, and I'm frequently worried I don't have language to describe what I'm doing or what I want to do. Finally, beyond the language or the scholarship, in some ways I feel like committing to community work is an exercise in learning that one has only momentary successes in the midst of glaring, obvious failure.

In confronting that resistance, I think I remained hesitant because I did not know how I would describe the roles I imagined for scholars engaging local communities or how I would talk about strategies they might employ, because much of the scholarship I found presented a very different role for the scholar and a different orientation toward the work than any I might look to. Like a double-dutch jump-roper lurching toward the rope but never jumping, I avoided our disciplinary conversation on this subject because as Jackie Jones Royster might have put it, the first voices I heard were not my own. Thus, I ask in this chapter: What does the figure of the digital griot offer scholars struggling to figure out what role(s) they might play? What relationships might they build with communities? What rhetorical strategies might further their work? I argue here that while many committed teachers and scholars doing community work wonder how they might maintain an appropriate scholarly distance from communities and avoid being seen as identifying too closely with the aims or goals of the groups with which they work, sometimes—and particularly for some African American scholars—such avoidance is neither possible nor desired. Articulations of the scholar's relationship to community and to community work as that of a griot may offer a more appropriate role and some guidance as to how to pursue it. After considering the tensions that exist for African American scholars doing community work and presenting the digital griot as a figure that can inform the roles, relationships, and rhetorical strategies scholars might pursue, I will talk through how I have attempted to put these ideas to work in my own community teaching—not to present it as a model for anyone else, but rather just to share how I have tried to find my way, find my mix.

The challenges of figuring out how a scholar who hopes to engage local communities can envision his or her role in that work is sometimes beyond daunting. Of course there are the practical considerations of how one balances the many demands of adjunct or graduate assistant or tenure track jobs when one's livelihood is by no means secure—or securable through community work. But the debates around how one might engage such work are more than enough to make one simply become resigned to watching the rope turn. As teachers and scholars with a certain outlook on the world, we have a sense of what kind of work is important, what issues we care about, and our implicit or explicit theories of what literacy work can or should do. We know that we are not alone, however, and that the communities we hope to collaborate with must find value in any work we might propose to do, which leads to a more-than-delicate balancing act of building relationships and dialogue with multiple, sometimes conflicting stakeholders all while developing the political skills and savvy to understand how these figures and organizations operate in any local context. As if the time and rhetorical skill to build relationships with these entities, to understand how they all operate in a given locale, and to get a handle on the internal debates over what might be needed were not enough, there remain very difficult disciplinary, departmental, and institutional terrains to be navigated. Even in a department and institution where community work is valued or even central to their missions, this navigation is enough to make one wanna holler, as Marvin Gaye would say.

My own institution has been involved in all of these complexities since our current chancellor, Nancy Cantor, arrived and presented a rearticulation of Syracuse University's vision as one of "Scholarship in Action." Engagement with local communities through an understanding of the goal of intellectual work as one of contributing to a common good and a commitment to social justice has been refreshing. Watching some of the backlash that followed her arrival as either outright rejection in some quarters or genuine concern and debate over what such a vision might look like or even utter confusion over how to implement such a vision even if people answered the call has been less so. The old line about not wanting to watch sausage being made is applicable here, as all of the institutional grinding taking place in the debates over conceptualization and implementation often reinforced my desire to pursue community work independently of my job and accept whatever support my department or college or university might be able to offer such work but never ask for it. And I felt like I should, at all costs, keep my own thoughts about the roles and purposes of community work as far away as possible from the institutional grinding and sausage-making that were so disconcerting to me. Of course, this grinding is not the result of right versus wrong, progressive versus conservative, or obstinate people intentionally hindering whatever I and some others might consider "progress" but is often instead a result of genuine disagreement and dialogue across competing sets of values where people on all sides see themselves as working toward some sense of a broader public good.

David Coogan offers a compelling treatment of the complex roles, expectations, and audiences present for scholars attempting to do community literacy work. He also argues convincingly for a scholarly caution, for the maintenance of a kind of distance from local communities in the name of preserving intellectual inquiry as one's main goal. In his article "Community Literacy as Civic Dialogue," he presents an intergenerational oral history project he developed with residents of a black neighborhood in Chicago and his students. The tension, as he reports it, emerges from problems that develop when teacher-scholars are linked too closely to the communities with which they work. If we are not careful, community members, students, and teachers can be tied down to a narrow sense of purpose when we identify too closely with notions of the "struggle." Such close identification with the community and with its struggles (in this case, of the African American community in Chicago with which Coogan worked, with *the* struggle), especially when one takes up advocacy as a part of his or her stated goals, can result in a "tethering" of the visions and expectations of scholars, students, and residents to simplistic narratives that lead us to miss the depth and complexity of the lives and stories of community members we claim we want to collaborate with and serve. When confronted by questions, and even skepticism, from community activists who wondered how this oral history project might actually benefit that community, Coogan responded:

> I readily understood much could be gained from constituting a community in struggle. I also realized that much could be lost or flattened in that characterization. . . . Those discourses, including advocacy, may sometimes cultivate that indifference

when they place the requirements of identification ahead of the opportunity to do inquiry. When that happens, I believe we need to hold advocacy in abeyance a little while and create a space for civic dialogue. (96)

While he worked carefully in his undergraduate course to teach students about the "struggle" of African Americans in Southside Chicago and in the larger nation, in framing his oral history project and describing its aims to local activists, he "contradicted their vision of a 'struggling community'" (96). Resisting close identification with community and advocacy as a goal for community service work, Coogan posits "civic dialogue" as a corrective. By imagining a role and a position for scholars and students doing community work on the other end of a continuum from advocacy and identification, Coogan believes those involved in community literacy work can ensure the importance of inquiry and prevent simplistic assumptions about a local community. Preventing these assumptions and "flattening" narratives can, in his opinion, allow for richer dialogue among all of the collaborators and still foster critical dialogue that is not "present-bound by an agenda, vocabulary, and identification with an issue or movement" (107).

Coogan links his argument about the role scholars and students pursuing community work should seek to Deweyan ideals about progressive education and specifically to Celeste Condit's important essay "The Character of 'History' in Rhetoric and Cultural Studies" to call for a distinction between the "activist" and the "politically progressive academic" who can stand apart from direct identification with causes and communities in order to foster broader inquiry and dialogue. As convincing as his (and Condit's) arguments are, and as valuable as the stories he and his students collected are and the inquiry that emerged with local residents surely is, I'm reminded of so many of the other books and articles I've read, reminded of my initial resistance to entering the dialogue. I remained lurching toward the rope turning but never wanting to enter because I needed (and need) a different rhythm, a different cadence, some different voices.

To be honest about my own biases, I need a different role or model because I believe and represent much of what Coogan passionately cautions against. Much of that resistance I hold toward some of the scholarly discourse on community literacy comes from the fact that I do care, I do *identify*, I do believe in advocacy, and I long knew I could never pretend to hold any of the objectivity or scholarly detachment (at least in this area) that academic writing so often requires. That is especially the case with my own efforts at community work. I am too invested in the project, in the people who have come together over the last six years, and in the joys, struggles, visions, and histories of this community to fake either objectivity or reserve. Service or community work emanating from, to, and with the academy can never fully represent this ideal, but I believe that such work has to be about communities and students and scholars coming together to genuinely build together. The one-way model of a professor taking his or her "expertise" to some audience that professor has decided could benefit from it has its place, but it was never my place or my way. Where so much (though not all, by any means) work on community writing or community literacy followed this one-way model of going into specific communities to build writing or literacy skills, I wanted to use writing and literacy to build community. So the ends for me were never fully writing and/ or literacy, as important as they are as intermediate goals. It's always been about trying to create some different kind of space—that living room, if you will—where everyone is at home and where we can all be engaged, all be challenged, to move on up a little higher, as Mahalia Jackson would say. A space where we are all free to imagine and work toward a community somehow changed, a world somehow different, even as we remain clear that the work of transformation takes generations.

So while Coogan's use of civic dialogue and the "rivaling" that Lorraine Higgins, Elenore Long, and Linda Flower present as a model for community literacy based on their work in Pittsburgh and Ellen Cushman's use of everyday rhetorical practices in the filling out of housing and employment applications are all appropriate, rhetorically based approaches to community literacy work, my problem of "identification" and my desire to use literacy work to build community rather than the other way around led me to search for other alternatives and ultimately to the figure of the griot as a way to understand the role of the scholar-activist and the rhetorical strategies I need to hone in order to use literacy work to build community, build with community, and at times advocate for local communities.

Beverly Moss and Manning Marable each invoke the figure of the griot in community literacy and in any kind of work engaging local communities. Moss's book *A Community Text Arises* is one of the most powerful statements on the subject by anyone in the discipline of composition, contending that literacy is not about individuals somehow in relationship with surrounding contexts but is truly a community endeavor, a collaborative endeavor. In this way, she points toward different understandings of the relationships scholars might develop with local communities. Where Moss directs me toward possibility and a sense of additional rhetorical strategies one might bring to this kind of work, Marable in *Living Black History* troubles the waters in a very different direction by challenging black scholars toward an utterly impossible—though utterly necessary—understanding of the role of scholarship, one that resists easy narratives about quantifiable successes and simple connections to university, foundation, or other institutional goals.

Moss's book is masterful for her redefinition of literacy as fundamentally about community and collaboration, but it is also important for the work she does, like Royster does in *Traces of a Stream*, and like Diana Cardenas does in her valuable essay "Creating an Identity: Personal, Academic, and Civic Literacies," in addressing the always present double- and multiple-consciousness that black scholars, Latino/a scholars, and other academics of color face at the intersections of scholarly and personal identity. These tensions can be especially pronounced when one commits to community work: almost every scholar of color I know in our field and many beyond it have entered the academy explicitly, have consciously pursued academic work out of a desire to serve their home communities as well as the academy. Many African American scholars enter the academy deeply aware of the fact that our accomplishments and ability to complete doctoral degrees are not individual achievements but community accomplishments and with an intense desire to serve those communities whose known and unknown members bore us up and got us over. Like Sethe confronting Stamp Paid at the river in Toni Morrison's *Beloved*, they, we, know that our passage was paid for before we got to the river. After identifying a set of research interests that helped her resolve these tensions, Moss describes the feeling common to many this way:

> Yet here, seemingly, was an opportunity to do research in a setting that would allow me *to be who I was*—an African American woman who can normally be found in church on a Sunday morning. As important, I had the opportunity to do research in a setting—African American churches—that would extend the discussion on literacy acquisition and literate practices among African Americans. (2, emphasis added)

So many scholars, including African American scholars, search diligently for ways to pursue research agendas that will have some kind of benefit for the communities who paid and paved the way for their presence in the academy.

Beyond bearing witness to Moss's discussion of the search for research questions and agendas and methods that helped her traverse the disconnect between town and gown, hill and hood, however, I am most interested in the ways in which *A Community Text Arises* extends social literacies scholarship to move past considerations of individuals as social learners and toward an understanding of literacy as being a truly community-based endeavor. The literate practices she describes and the deeply layered relationships that exist between multiple practices and multiple participants, more than maybe any other work in our field, helped me envision how I might pursue community literacy work.

Neither the idea that African Americans have deep, "rich and complex literacy and language activity occurring in the home communities of these racial and ethnic groups" (Moss 3) nor the fact that there are gaps between these literacy practices and those we teach and reward in school nor even the thought that these practices and the traditions from which they emerge could be powerful bridges for educators is new in our field—though we all need continual reminders of these points, and Moss offers these reminders compel-lingly. In fact, each of these three notions is somewhat commonly held among many literacy scholars (at least in theory, if not always in praxis), including quite a few in rhetoric and composition. The innovation in Moss's study that holds such import for me, and I believe for community work, is her description of the ways in which call and response and other rhetorical strategies are used collabora-tively by African Americans in the creation of community spaces, texts, and literacies. The point she develops throughout the book is that this collaboration is not simply one of the call and response that takes place during the sermon to make the sermon a collaboratively authored text but that all of the texts and activities of the worship service and the day-to-day life of the church—and the community outside the church—come together. Literacy becomes "a complex, social process involving multiple levels of participation by rhetors and audience, intertextual relationships (i.e., *interdependent* relationships between oral, written, and sometimes musical texts) and complex belief systems of members of particular communities" (6, emphasis added). In other words, the acquisition of literacies and the texts produced depend not simply on the existence of these multiple fac-tors but on their interaction at the same time and over time:

> The social nature of literacy requires that there are multiple participants in this process . . . that is, there is not a solitary writer nor an isolated reader; writer and reader collaborate in the act of making the text. The writer and reader also share the roles of speaker and listener, making the levels of participation more complex. . . . The roles are interchangeable, and without this unique role reversal, the text as it comes into being in African American churches would not exist. (7)

Two issues that this observation presents for the educator or com-munity worker are that (1) the script constantly gets flipped, and one must prepare for and even welcome a kind of role reversal that will both challenge and affirm any sense of authority we might bring to teaching, and (2) as she cites from the highly respected black homiletician Henry H. Mitchell, "one must preach in the idiom of the people" (25). Thus, one must have a teaching voice, an activist voice, a scholarly voice that allows one to teach, politic, build, act, plan, in the idiom of the people—whoever "the people" are in the settings in which we hope to work. And one must teach in the idiom—not just the language practices but the ways of seeing the world, the ways of being in the world, the values, attitudes, knowledge, needs, hopes, joys, and contributions of a people as expressed through their language.

One important point in Moss's study as she describes the interaction of many actors and texts in the collaborative construction of literacy is her recognition that seemingly innocuous literacy events are crucial to the building of the community: moments in the church setting like the responsive readings of scripture, greetings and the reading of announcements, the individual congregants' readings and discussions of the church bulletin during and after service, the welcoming of visitors, the songs played and sung, affirmations, testimonies, and more—these routine activities are crucial to the overall literacy event because they contribute to the building of shared knowledge. One of the pastors Moss studies combines a paraphrasing of Mitchell's call to preach in the idiom of the people with the importance of building shared knowledge in a literacy community by saying, "People want the preacher to 'bring it to me in a cup I can recognize'" (80). One of the most important jobs of the preacher, teacher, griot, scholar, then, is to be able to connect with the audience "where they are" (80). This use of shared knowledge by the griot works in at least two ways: first, through call and response, it allows the audience to participate in the construction of knowledge and thus creates a more equal relationship with the preacher/teacher/ scholar. And second, using shared knowledge also helps to contribute to the creation of new knowledge: "using the familiar—the shared knowledge—to teach the unfamiliar is an effective way of teaching a people about their culture, their heritage" (98). Moss exemplifies this strategy in action by presenting one of the ministers who used the Lord's Prayer and specifically built on the phrase "Our Father" in a segment of a sermon to teach congregants about traditional African faith systems:

In African religions God is called the one who exists by himself
And he is called the one who is met everywhere
He is called the great ocean headdress in the horizon
And he is called the wise one
The all seeing the one who brings round the seasons
The Zulu calls him he who bends down even majesties
The Zulu call him the irresistible
The Bankutu speak of him as Nzambi
The Yoruba call him Olaroon
The Ashanti call him Neonmi

(98)

Moss identifies several rhetorical strategies that are a part of the process of building community and building literacy through shared knowledge: call and response, code switching, collective "we," and extending boundaries through shared knowledge (92). Among the most important of these strategies, and one that perhaps most directly calls up the figure of the griot, is that of building knowledge through narrative sequencing. Geneva Smitherman defines narrative sequencing as a central strategy in black rhetorical traditions, as a strategy of building knowledge and making arguments through the telling of stories. In the words of Reverend M., one of the pastors Moss studies, "Black folk relate to stories; they don't want that logical, syllogistic form. . . . It's part of our heritage. It goes back to the Griots" (115). One final rhetorical strategy that the preacher as griot must employ is identification. He or she not only must be able to tell *the* story but also must be willing to share *his or her* story in order to create a relationship with the audience. Moss cites Henry Mitchell to make this point: "Authority was granted to the ministers by the congregation because the ministers demonstrated that they could provide personal testimony to what God had done for them" (142). She again quotes Mitchell to say that "it must be clear that the minister is filled by the same joy he declares to his congregation. If indeed the preacher has not tasted and seen that it is good, he has nothing, really, to say" (142). Moss continues to relate that this identification is not merely a matter of bearing witness to the value of God—or, for this conversation, of scholarship or intellectual work—but says that one is able to "show that they, too, had struggled just like members of the congregation. The ministers could speak for themselves and the congregation at the same time because of their shared experiences; the ministers' struggles were the people's struggles," and the narrative, the story, is the way in which the links of those common struggles are forged for knowledge building and future work (143).

These processes of collaboration and identification, of call and response and building shared knowledge, of code switching, finding, and using shared language, for Moss lead to the creation of a shared text. In other words, the preacher is no longer a sole author, and the congregation can no longer be said to play the role of mere listener or receiver. They create the text together. In some ways, one might argue the sermon becomes a kind of communal wiki—community property—because the text changes all the time as the preaching moment changes and audience members make their direct and indirect contributions.

The lessons for educators, as Moss presents them, are several: that literacy work must become communal instead of narrowly focused on individual learners, that the cultural knowledge and expectations of learners must be central to any instruction, that we must use the rhetorical practices of students and community members to build bridges between non-school and academic literacy practices (157), and, perhaps most important, that we must change the role of teacher and student and create roles for audiences to create the "text" of learning with us. The griot's role as community-based or community-engaged scholar is not to "break 'em off" with all he or she knows or even to "break it down" as if the griot has all the knowledge relative to a given situation but to create conditions where a community creates its own collaborative text. Thus community literacy work, if we learn anything from the griotic role of the preacher, is to wiki with the audience. The teaching voice, the pedagogy, the content—just like Moss's study of the sermon—help build a community text that emerges from everyday activities and interactions.

Where Moss uses the griotic role of the black preacher to present compelling analysis of the social processes and communal dynamics of literacy and several of the rhetorical strategies that emerge from such a collaborative, communal pursuit of literacy, Marable calls on the griot to challenge black scholars toward different understandings of history and of the roles scholars can and should play in building community and in collaborations with those communities. Marable positions his essay "Living Black History: Resurrecting the African American Intellectual Tradition" at the beginning of a section called "Rethinking Black Studies" in his book *Great Wells of Democracy* as a challenge to black scholars, arguing that at a time when formal restrictions on black participation in American society were shrinking, black studies scholarship as a whole and many intellectuals connected to the "tradition" remained aloof with respect to the struggles of the masses of black people. After noting long-standing critiques of the black middle class from Frantz Fanon and Malcolm X, Marable notes:

> Black public intellectuals in the age of racial revolution saw their scholarship as contributing to a building of a necessary intellectual rationale for the destruction of legal structured racism. Ironically, during the past quarter century, as legal barriers and restrictions on racial advancement in many respects have come down, the overall character of black studies scholarship is largely disengaged with the problems of the urban poor. Today's elitist discourse of liberal multiculturalism speaks the safe language of symbolic representation, but rarely of resistance. Our scholarship indeed must be rigorous and objective, but if it lacks vision or is not informed in its substructure by *passionate collective memory*, how meaningful can it be to the one million African Americans who currently are incarcerated in this nation's correctional facilities? Glittering public intellectuals may appear to offer a depth of social commentary in the media, but too frequently their politics and comprehension of history have shallow roots. (9, emphasis added)

By dissing the shallow shine he perceives in many black public intellectuals, Marable calls for a different relationship to history and to community and for work with and on behalf of the community than is possible for scholars whose work is measured in the seconds of television or radio sound bites or the fleeting moments of exposure granted to communities through the five-figure sums plus honoraria many such scholars receive for hour-long speeches. By quoting theorist Antonio Gramsci and looking to people like Malcolm X, C. L. R. James, Frantz Fanon, and W. E. B. Du Bois as models, Marable argues for a lifelong commitment by black scholars rooted in community rather than in media who see themselves as "constructor, organiser, permanent persuader and not just a simple orator" (Gramsci qtd. in Marable 6). This role of permanent persuader must be defined by vision and grounded in "passionate collective memory."

The griotic role for activist scholars, for Marable, has two elements: a commitment to fundamental social transformation, which is the purpose that guides their work (7), and a relationship to history and memory. In the black scholar's relationship to history and community, Marable's model becomes the time binder that Alondra Nelson, Ishmael Reed, and Ivan Van Sertima see as the griot's function: one who lives with the ancestors and their stories, one who walks with the "living dead," understanding that "the social weight of the ancestors frequently transcends the physical boundaries of life and death, as narrowly defined in the West" (9). Ultimately, just as Nelson, Reed, and Tom Hale argue, Marable asserts that the scholar as griot must actively seek to create Papa LaBas's future text: "The Black intellectual must *actively* engage the past in such a way that it tends to obliterate the boundaries that appear to divide the past from the present, and from the future" (9).

By presenting the role of the scholar as Gramsci's "permanent persuader," Marable offers a vision of the griot that is not just a collector of stories or a bearer of a community's history but one who uses that history, that passionate collective memory, that rememory, in the pursuit of a new present and future. The scholar as griot, as "living historian,"

> is obligated to become a civic actor, as innovative knowledge collected and drawn from the past shapes important legislative

initiatives and enriches public school curricula. The goal is
not just to educate and inform, but to transform the objective
material and cultural conditions and subordinate status of marginalized groups, through informed civic engagement, and by
strengthening civil society. In effect, we attempt to reconstruct
America's memory about itself, and our collective past. (11)

Time binder. Permanent persuader. Civic actor. One who actively
works to build community, works with community, speaks to and, at
times, on behalf of community. Committed to the poor. Willing to
resist. Working toward transformation rather than reform. Marable's
standard for the scholar looking to build with community would
seem to be an impossible one, and certainly a daunting one, especially for members of a group of scholars who only recently, and only
tentatively, have been welcomed into the academy at all. But neither
career success nor success in specific community work is the point.
Rather, one's commitment to the task is the issue. A point James
Cone makes in his critique of the black church is instructive here.
At the 2007 State of Black America forum in a session specifically
focused on the black church and its relationships to the communities it serves, Cone made it finally make sense to me when he said:

I feel today that with so much focus on building buildings
and all the other humongous things we do, that we fail to see
that the cross is at the heart of what the Black church ought
to be about. It was not very difficult for the Black church to
see that during the time in which it was born, because being
a slave church, that was not success. It was obvious failure
there. Now the problem is that the church has lost its legacy,
has lost its message, and when success becomes the focus of
it, it loses its mission, and loses its message. I would like to
see the church not be so concerned with success, and more
concerned with a kind of ultimate success through failure.
("State of Black America 2007")

Cone's words to the audience at the State of Black America gathering
address the question of purpose and challenged the crowd to pursue

the impossible, struggle with the big issues, and work in the interest of service rather than success.

Before discussing how Moss, Marable, Cone, and the griot came to inform my vision of community-engaged scholarship or describing my version of a digital griot writing curriculum for a community audience, I should tell a little bit of the story—in order to provide some background, to share the journey, and to highlight some of the voices that made this work a real and growing community text and mix—of the community text that arose from the project I began. There's a little of my own story, a little of the internal conversation with some of my colleagues that helped provide a spark for this work, and some love for—and many shoutouts to—the hundreds of people who have been a part of this effort. A caveat here: Cone's words about success really do fit my thoughts about this project. I make no claims toward the kinds of results that academics and administrators often yearn to see. Dropout rates in Syracuse have not fallen; test scores have not risen. We have not come up with new and innovative ways to address AIDS and HIV or homelessness, nor have we dismantled the prison industrial complex. We still struggle with the violence that destroys young lives and traumatizes families and neighborhoods in Syracuse. We have not increased literacy according to any of the measurable indices that are often used. But we have created a space where we can all lower ourselves more deeply into the beauty, pain, joy, struggle, and genius of black traditions and contemporary experiences, or as Marable would say, into those great wells of democracy, dug deep by our ancestors, to gather up our strength and abilities to do the long, hard work of individual, community, and global transformation. And while we avoid any grand claims about victories or success, the time we have spent tarrying in those traditions has brought about many small and medium successes. Small pockets of people in Syracuse, and sometimes larger ones, see intellectual work as activist work and have had their ideas and visions confirmed and challenged. People within and beyond the courses have begun to engage the depth and complexity of African American traditions and to explore the lessons those traditions hold for the future of African American struggle and for our entire society, a society that often utterly fails to recognize that depth and complexity.

Since my childhood, and especially since my early days as an undergraduate at Cleveland State University, involved in a student protest of the firing of Dr. Raymond Winbush as the university's Vice President for Minority Affairs, I was a part of a community that wanted intellectual work to be more than just explicating, obfuscating, and pontificating. Those of us involved in that protest, from dear friends like John R. Walton, Darren Carter, and Stanley Gordon to many of the elders from the university and community who supported us with their wisdom and their work—people like Pat Washington and Frank Adams and Curtis Wilson and Mwatabu Okantah and Norma Jean Freeman and Don Freeman and Charles Bevel—all yearned for a university that was committed to intellectual rigor and to using that rigor to make some kind of difference for the families and neighborhoods from which we came. Many of my own commitments to what teaching and learning should be were forged in that crucible: as much as I admired (and still do admire) the work of people like Cornel West, Michael Eric Dyson, bell hooks, Adolph Reed, Kimberle Crenshaw, Robin Kelley, and Derrick Bell, the role of the public intellectual never appealed much to me. Especially now that I'm in the academy, the role of the public intellectual seems to me something like that of the preacher: in many black churches across the country, any young man (the church still isn't comfortable encouraging women to see themselves in the pulpit) who could put two sentences together is encouraged, even expected, to "accept the call" to ministry. The academy seems to be the same way: any brother or sister with a PhD and some kind of personality is encouraged and expected to take on the public intellectual role. And it is an important role, given the lack of access African Americans still have to public forums and political spaces.

The kind of intellectual wreck that West, Reed, Crenshaw, Julianne Malveaux, and others bring in the impossible spaces of corporatized media and publishing is absolutely crucial to our interests. However, I always knew I wasn't made in that mold. I couldn't do what they do if I wanted to. But not only that—it always bothered me that the people who might be the most encouraged by their work often never get to see it. Even with the scholars in our field, the only way most will read the crucial work of those whose shoulders I stand on—Keith Gilyard, Geneva Smitherman, Jackie Royster, Shirley Wilson Logan, Elaine Richardson, and Gwen Pough—is if they enroll in an undergraduate elective (maybe) or graduate seminar. Even for those who have greater media coverage, people like Kelley and West and Crenshaw, so many in the "community" hear them or even hear of them only in the sound bite. Given this problem, I began to see myself more and more as someone who would try to carry their work beyond the television or the occasional newspaper reference—carry it to those who needed to read it, hear it, be challenged and encouraged by it.

So I always imagined trying to do something on local levels, even underground levels, to try to take intellectual work to the people themselves, in home spaces rather than through the media and lecture circuit. I imagined a space where the vernacular and the theoretical came together and where both would be taken seriously. As a graduate student at Penn State, impressed with the kind of work Richardson did with black students at State College High School (work she never sought credit or accolades or publications for), I would imagine a course here and there that I might try to teach whenever I made it to the other side. But this journey had far less ambitious beginnings.

A big part of this—part of my awkward attempts to put community work into conversation with larger department and university conversations—began with me trying to get out of some work rather than do some work. I had been thinking about trying to do something in Syracuse's African American community throughout my first year on the faculty, but my thoughts were pretty scattered and unorganized—and un-acted on at that point. During the summer before my second year at Syracuse, one of my senior colleagues was directing a small grant focused on diversity and writing instruction. The grant was organized around the idea of "working groups" of faculty, PWIs (professional writing instructors), and graduate students examining some important issue related to diversity and writing instruction and then planning events or work to bring that knowledge to the rest of our department. The grant's director wanted me to put together one of these working groups, and I had absolutely no interest in complying. I had a manuscript to finish revising, courses to plan. I didn't feel like I knew the department's or grant's politics well enough, and honestly, I didn't know if I could trust the intentions or the goals of those who were involved in the grant to really try to create some change in our curriculum and our department. I liked them well enough and didn't distrust them—I just didn't know that I could trust all of that enough yet to get involved in something so time-consuming, as I wasn't even in my second year yet in my first tenure-track job. So I told her no. I had no interest in getting involved in this grant and definitely no interest in running the unwieldy structure of some working group with people I'd choose but didn't yet know. I thought I was done with it, but the grant's principal investigator wasn't hearing it. She asked again; I said no again.

She invited me out for lunch, and guessing that the conversation would come up again, I thought I had the answer that would get her to leave me alone. I told her that I had reconsidered and would be glad to do something for the grant but that I had to be free to do whatever I wanted to do, no strings attached. I had to be free to ditch the working group structure and spend that small pot of money my way. Just when I was prepared for her to laugh at me and tell me I had a lot of nerve, rookie professor that I was, stepping out of pocket like that, she asked me what I had in mind. I proposed a course geared to Syracuse's African American community and designed to build dialogue between campus and community. To what was my initial dismay, she liked the idea and committed to supporting it. I never got to ditch the working group structure the first time around, but I had a little money to do what I wanted to do—and the challenge to produce. Of course, this conversation took place right before the start of the school year, and for all of the time I had spent thinking about teaching a community course and trying to build with Syracuse's local community, I was frozen. I had no idea how I'd get something off the ground in time and even less idea how I'd make it successful. But my hole card had been pulled, so I was going to have to represent . . .

Slow jam lover that I am, and "old school" music fan that I am, I had been wanting to do something connecting soul and funk to cultural and political issues. As far as I was concerned, there were people all over the place writing about Hip Hop, writing about jazz and the blues—there was plenty of conversation in the academy, and sometimes conversation that connected each of those genres to ideas about black culture, identity, and activism. I wanted to see something different, and the "old school" ethos that was a big part of popular culture gave me the perfect opportunity. Everybody was claiming to be old school, from the grownfolks' and elders' generations reaching back to Al Green and Etta James and Aretha Franklin and Motown and Stax to reclaim elements of African American identity and culture they were afraid were being lost in the Hip Hop generation, to those Hip Hoppers themselves, with their throwback jerseys and so-called classic shoes and samples in their music. But the connection went beyond the polemic of a generational split: there was also the neo-soul crew, who loved artists like D'Angelo and Angie Stone and Jill Scott and Kindred the Family Soul and many more because of their intentional reclamation of soul and funk as answers to the excesses of Hip Hop and a desire to connect in more meaningful ways with the culture and ideals of community and collective struggle.

So the music I loved long before I was old enough to know anything about what the Manhattans or Etta James or Donny Hathaway were actually talking about and the issues I hoped to engage people in conversation about—the repairing of communities, the search for answers to the huge questions that face us—came together, and I had the topic for my first course: What's Goin' On? The Music, Culture, and Politics of the Soul Era. I had no idea whether this effort would be successful or if I'd be sitting alone in some space talking to myself every Tuesday night, but I had an approach and some goals in mind, and I was ready to try it.

Before describing the courses further, I should say something about the commitments I brought to this effort, even from the beginning. I began the first community course unsure about many things, but I was also clear about some of what I was up to. I knew that I wanted this effort geared specifically to Syracuse's black community, that I wanted to create a comfortable space that took people's intellectual gifts and their concern about larger issues as givens, and that I wanted the class to be a place where everyone felt supported and encouraged. I also knew that I didn't want it to be a "program" or anything official, or even anything that was about huge amounts of publicity. In essence, I wanted it to be a "free space," intellectual and playful, committed and relaxed, challenging and supportive. To that end, I made some specific decisions about how I would approach this.

First, I decided that I would base the community course on a class I was teaching on campus. There were a few major reasons for this. Most important for me, I wanted something that was not based on the "skills" model of literacy in any way. I wanted to make it clear that the course and I took people's knowledge and abilities seriously. I also wanted the idea of the course to challenge people—to let them know that we'd be involved and engaged and that they would be stimulated.

Second, I wanted to focus on Syracuse's black community but also to foster dialogue between campus and community about African American culture, traditions, and futures. I imagined something developing where I would teach community courses but would also have events on campus and off and, eventually, people from the community would sit in my campus classes and vice versa. To understand why this was so important to me, a tangent is appropriate. One of my favorite movies in high school and during my undergrad years was Spike Lee's *School Daze*. Among the most compelling scenes in Lee's exploration of education and the ruptures it either helps create or expose in black communities involves a clash between the "Mission Men," led by Laurence Fishburne's character, Dap, and the neighborhood fellas, led by Samuel L. Jackson's character. The conflict emerges in the most everyday setting, lunch at a fast-food restaurant. While there are real material issues of employment and money and the psychic effects of despair that drive the resentment the neighborhood fellas feel toward the Mission Men, a major source of the beef comes from the sense that those students from the college are wrapped up in that missionary ideal, that condescension and arrogance that leaves some educated people caring deeply for their people but removed from them at the same time.

Syracuse has had the same kind of history in its black community, as have countless cities and towns all over the country. Blackfolk around town call Syracuse University "the Hill" and, until the arrival of our current chancellor, Nancy Cantor, saw the university as completely divorced from the town and its issues, save for the athletic teams. And whether fair or not, this perception extended to the African American faculty, staff, and students on campus as well. The sense that black students and academics don't care enough to genuinely engage the communities around us runs thick in Syracuse and many other places, as does the perception that black students and academics are ostracized because of their academic pursuits. In some small way, I wanted to close that gap, to help us all remind each other of how deeply we are connected to each other, no matter what the perceptions or stereotypes or realities might have been in the past.

Third, I did not want the course to feel like any of the official "programs" that usually result when universities or governmental or nonprofit institutions become involved in community work. Those efforts, even when well executed, often feel too clinical and carry too much of the gaze of the bureaucrat or so-called expert. In other words, it becomes far too easy to create situations where the participants aren't true participants at all but rather objects, recipients, clients. My ideal arrangement was a scenario that recreated agency by recreating community. And for me, this scenario had to be informal, relaxed. This need guided several of the choices I made. First, and perhaps most important, was the location. I needed a space that felt homey and, to some extent, underground. Public libraries wouldn't work for what I wanted; neither would "organization" spaces—community centers, churches, agencies, or schools. Too clinical, too clean. Some of this concern had to do with the actual physical spaces available more than the organization of these spaces: the design and layout and atmosphere of many of them simply didn't feel quite right, so the issue was both one of design and location. I needed a space that was both clean and funky, Saturday night and Sunday morning. I also needed the space to be *in* the community, both physically and psychically.

I resolved these issues by going to the jook joint: a restaurant/bar/club on Syracuse's south side called The Groove, thanks to a suggestion and encouragement from one of the first people I met in Syracuse, Chuck Jones. In many ways it was perfect: not only was it in the heart of Syracuse's black community, but it was black-owned and had a separate meeting space with tables and chairs that could be arranged as needed (space that doubled as the dance floor on weekends). And they served food, something any event planner knows is crucial, especially since I held the classes after work, from 6 to 8, on Tuesday nights. The owners were supportive of us, and we were able to support an African American business. And even more important, the restaurant/club type of space invited people to hang around and commune after class sessions, a fact that did more to build relationships and create the kind of comfort level that made the classes special than I could have imagined.

My priorities for the kind of space and experience I wanted these classes to be and become influenced many other decisions I made as well. One of those decisions had to do with how to publicize the courses, especially on the short notice of the first course, having had only three weeks to publicize it before it was scheduled to begin. A side note: my decision to present courses based on my campus classes meant that I had to more or less follow the academic calendar, so my pattern has been to start the community courses two weeks after the start of the campus semester. This allows me a buffer in publicizing the courses, and, I believe, keeps the courses' length manageable for people who also work, lead families, and have spouses and partners and social lives and many other commitments. But because this first course was geared to African Americans and because my goal was to create community through it, many of the usual means would not work. Newspapers and television and the Internet would not do: I had to go where the people were. I had to make sure they saw me and got to talk to me, ask questions, wonder what on earth I was up to. In essence, the community had to know I wanted to be there, that this would not be some "program" or some distant effort by somebody "up there on the Hill."

Given these needs, I had to get into the underground. I had two main approaches to spreading the word for the courses. I went back to my undergraduate days of fraternities and sororities and Hip Hop groups and DJs publicizing parties. I made flyers and hit the streets. I couldn't get around the town as much as I wanted to in the three weeks I had (one week before the start of the semester), but I went to the barbershops, to the beauty shops, to black businesses on the south side of Syracuse. I went to supermarkets and even to the mall once or twice handing flyers out to whatever blackfolk I saw. And even though I did not want to use mass media, I went to the "old school" or "grownfolks" radio station and recorded a public service announcement. I had three versions of the flyers for the first course: two different black and white handbills and one color poster, all designed by Don Sawyer, a staff member in SU's Office of Student Affairs who has been incredibly supportive of this work, whose knowledge of history, ability to "tell it," and technological skills truly make him one of those digital griots who helped me to shape my thoughts about what writing for, in, and with community can be.

My strategy for this first course was rooted in Amiri Baraka's reflection that we are a "blues people"—that black music traditions are powerful and important sites of memory, engagement, identity formation, and even activism. I organized the course around the soul era to try to tap into this observation, hoping to use the music as a bridge to engage larger issues of culture, politics, and activism. One could say I rather consciously employed a rhetoric of nostalgia, too, tapping into the "old school" ethos that has operated over the last ten to fifteen years (which I explore in the next chapter) as not only a reclamation of soul and funk music but also a searching through that music for values, mores, and commitments of what now seems to have been a better time. Before Hip Hop artists and large corporations tried to jack the old school ethos with throwback jerseys and sneakers and cola commercials (and still, in spite of that jacking), people claimed they were old school because they yearned for a return to large-scale black activism, for stable families, for a feeling of cultural unity, for a world before AIDS and the ravages of deindustrialization. I appealed to that ethos not only because I knew people would enjoy exploring old school music but also in hopes of evoking that sense of possibility that people hope for when they reach back to that old school. I was appealing to the old school crowd or, as we would say, the grownfolks who did that reflecting back to the soul era: both the grownfolks who lived it—those elders who came of age during the civil rights and Black Power movements—and the emerging ones who, now in their twenties, thirties, and early forties, grew up with the songs and stories as the nation and black community underwent the major changes of the 1970s, 1980s, and 1990s. Of course, given my concern with recreating that "living room," part of my motivation was making sure people knew this effort would be both fun and intellectually stimulating.

There are two other reasons for this choice of a topic for the first class: since this would also have to be the topic for my campus class, I felt it lent itself well to both my teaching priorities and my desire to create dialogue between students and community members. It wasn't just the grownfolks and elders who would claim that they were old school, even though eighteen-year-olds, thirty-somethings, and elders often have very different ideas about what constitutes the old school. Also, my goal in the writing classroom has always been to make students aware of the possibilities and responsibilities in writing as social action—as engagement with issues in people's everyday lives as much as the broader, more abstract academic aims that often attend notions of first-year writing and other writing courses. So I saw this as a perfect opportunity to help my students gain some real rhetorical sensitivity through having to write to and respond to real audiences who would be in their world, even if they weren't on campus.

Finally, I chose the soul era as a site of inquiry for this first course 'cause I was signifyin a li'l bit because of the arrival of a new chancellor and president on our campus who had identified "exploring the Soul of Syracuse" as her inaugural theme. I had no idea who Nancy Cantor was initially, beyond the basics of her history at Michigan and Illinois and had no idea whether she really cared about community engagement or was merely another missionary who had found a language with some currency. So, in some small way, I meant for my course to challenge her language, to ask, however rhetorically, what she meant by "Soul of Syracuse." I wanted to bring the history, the bodies, the visions of those who lived the soul that I knew into the conversation, whether she had planned to or not. I later came to find out that Chancellor Cantor would be and has been committed to a vision of social justice and genuine intellectual and practical collaboration with community. But at the time I was a little suspicious—to the point where I rather brazenly, though just playfully enough, just deferentially enough for a rookie, untenured professor, asked her whether she meant to evoke the soul of Aretha and Stevie and Sam Cooke and Etta James and Black Power and civil rights in her inaugural theme or whether she just meant some general philosophical debate about the spirit or essence of something.

More detail follows about the individual classes and the relationships, events, and people who made this journey so much more than some classes, but these early details about the decisions I made and the approach that guided them are meant not only to make clear the commitments with which I began but also to give sense of the other voices that were involved in making even the first course happen, that were important parts of the mix.

What happened was . . . a course became a community. Groups as small as fifteen and as large as sixty-five made the courses much more than a class or some readings but a different kind of space and even a community of its own. As wonderful as the courses themselves were for me, the real beauty of this effort has been in the gifts, passions, and visions that members of the "Village Movement" brought and the ways they pushed us beyond anything I imagined we would do or be able to do. The clichéd thing to say at this point would be that I've learned so much more than members in the course possibly could have, but there is far more at work than their having or my having learned some things. We have built each other up, formed deep and powerful friendships, reached out to support other members of the Syracuse community, and begun some powerful initiatives together. Beyond the ten courses over six years, and everything that members have brought to make those courses a different kind of community space, there have been community celebrations, a book party, a father's funeral, a wedding, a road trip to the 2006 Conference on College Composition and Communication in Chicago, a community conference on race and technology, forums on the state of education for black students, visits by other scholars on African American language and oral traditions, a community dialogue recorded for radio (and celebration of the host's one-year anniversary of his radio show), mobilization for a judge who was treated unfairly, and a Saturday school for middle school students.

By sharing the details of what we have done and what we have experimented with, attempted, and sometimes played with in six years, I hope to make the case here for genuine community engagement—not as "programs" or "initiatives" but as the unofficial kinds of work that won't always fit into the official language of academic departments or grant makers or the academy's tenure and promotion reward structure and as a central part of the work we choose to do. There are several reasons to place such importance on this kind of work.

One important reason that, alone, is enough to challenge teachers and scholars beyond the service learning model of community work has to do with audience. Many teachers, students, and scholars in composition and rhetoric are genuinely concerned with community work and service; there is a commitment to democratic possibility that runs throughout our field that leads us to work diligently, to both theoretically and practically meet people where they are and deal with the realities of class, gender, race, sexuality, and the day-to-day issues that often get masked because of the analytical frameworks and theoretical questions we focus on as academics. In this commitment to finding ways to serve, however, we often get caught up in the old colonial missionary role. We often see ourselves as the experts who are going to take our skills and our messages about literacy to communities we have decided need the benefits that literacy can bring. We go out and preach the economic, political, and social advantages of literacy, of our approach to literacy, to convert those who don't yet believe and teach those who don't yet know.

Unfortunately, because this approach to service and to service learning is sometimes the dominant one, even sincere efforts at service create a one-way relationship that ultimately reinforces town/gown divides rather than reduces or eliminates them. And unfortunately, we're often placed in this bind by the machinery and politics we're forced to endure to get the resources it takes to do this work: funders want to see results, and they want to see quantifiable results with specific populations. However, every community has legions of people who touch the people we want to serve in those efforts. People who work for nonprofit agencies, current and retired educators, activists, people working in many other fields who look for a space in which to be more active: they want to be—and need to be—connected with the ideas and issues with which we struggle; they need intellectual stimulation and spaces to which they can bring their talents and visions.

Building meaningful, sustaining, two-way relationships between universities and communities requires something far more than the traditional one-way service model, even when there are pressing needs for those kinds of services. So one challenge for community work is the building of community itself by bringing people together in spaces that focus on sharing their gifts and visions and commitments rather than skills and by engaging them in the kinds of conversations that sustain and stimulate those gifts, visions, and commitments. The message here is that the university or the professor or the department is not the solution to the issues that face a community. The community is, and the job of one who would do community work is to create spaces where people can pursue those solutions together. This approach can often lead to colleagues and even community people wondering where the real action, where the real work, is—where the success is—but this frustration simply has to be seen as a part of the cost of doing this work. Community efforts focused on the missionary model and its attendant narratives of literacy work automatically being "transformative" not only risk further alienating that community but also ignore a critical audience that often goes unserved.

The first course, What's Goin' On? The Music, Culture, and Politics of the Soul Era, was an exploration of that "old school" ethos I mentioned earlier and its sources in an attempt to see how the ideas of this period still resonate—or do not resonate—with people in the issues with which they were concerned. We used three books in the course: Michael Eric Dyson's *Mercy, Mercy Me: The Art, Loves, and Demons of Marvin Gaye*, Craig Werner's *Higher Ground: Stevie Wonder, Aretha Franklin, Curtis Mayfield, and the Rise and Fall of American Soul*, and Mark Anthony Neal's *What the Music Said: Black Popular Music and Black Public Culture*. The common thread with each of these books, in spite of their different styles and subjects, was that the music of the soul era was far more than entertainment, that it represented a space of engagement between African Americans and each other, the larger nation, and the world around issues of love, justice, and the future of the society. Twenty people (fifteen of whom attended every week) from across all of central New York and across a wide range of social, educational, and economic spaces attended the course regularly from beginning to end, and as much as people enjoyed talking about the individual artists or broader themes in the music of the soul era, frequently our discussion moved from the old school to the new, from issues in the music, like Motown's crossover strategy as opposed to the Stax label's grittier approach, to questions of how people can come together to repair and rebuild community.

Those Tuesday night sessions were structured around a relatively free-flowing discussion of the sections of the books that often went from the texts to current events to history to cultural and political issues and back again. Sometimes I played music before, during, and after to set a relaxed or upbeat mood, and we would have food together at the end of the session, giving us a chance to linger and get to know each other beyond the "course." There were two major strains of conversation that grew from this course: one was a near-universal desire to see and be involved in more action to address the issues people saw affecting their local communities and the African American community in general, and the second was a kind of inter-rogation of the "golden age" view that has come to attend the soul era. My role in the class was more facilitator, even trickster, than teacher in the traditional sense. My only goals were to get people involved in the texts and in conversation with each other, whether that meant pitting ideas against each other, mocking disagreement with someone in order to provoke a response, or just joking from time to time to lighten the mood. The point was to keep a positive environment, where everyone knew that he or she would have room to speak and would be supported. The course concluded with a joint campus/community celebration organized as a "Soul of Syracuse Awards" recognition ceremony, something that the participants planned together as a way to call the university's and community's attention to everyday warriors who often aren't given their due. Approximately 150 people from throughout the campus and local communities attended this dinner and ceremony, and we recognized 11 individuals with awards presented from the group. In my mind, the message here was to extend the effort beyond those who would take a particular course to announce that we were attempting to create a new kind of space that would honor voices and work that are often ignored and to announce that the university would be a part of that honor and recognition.

The course was a mixed success in that we had wonderful dialogue from week to week and people were genuinely excited about the prospect of this new kind of course and community space; we moved through the books and course material well and kept people engaged in it. The class was a little more book-club-ish than I would have liked, however, because I was reluctant to ask people to write. That may sound odd, given that I teach writing and reside in a writing department, but I found myself very sensitive to the fact that people who came to the course worked and had families and often had high levels of anxiety about writing, and I probably felt concerned about messing up a good thing by making it too much like "school," with assignments and such. I really wanted to keep the informal nature of the group dynamic and just didn't feel comfortable asking the members to "do" anything. Some of that reluctance, I'm sure, also emerged from my not having come to voice with the group yet. I hadn't yet worked out ways to prompt writing activities that fit the flow, the personality of the group, and my attempts to create a relaxed, egalitarian space. In my desire to break down some of the hierarchies associated with education, I was committed to a model that had us all engage as peers, and asking people to write from week to week felt way too much like being the old fart of a teacher. I grew past this, but it was an issue in the first course.

Another issue was that we simply were not able to do some of the events that I had initially planned. I had technology workshops set up to help people learn to create their own blogs and Web sites and to explore digital technologies, but no one attended the first one. This is the result of a few factors, I believe, from people's schedules not leaving them room to attend something on a second night during the week to my inexperience at promoting activities like this—I hadn't sharpened my rhetorical game—to the fact that we had not done anything on campus yet, nothing to break down the informal barriers that can keep community members from feeling comfortable attending events and activities there when the university had done so much in previous years to reinforce those psychic barriers.

Many of these issues resolved themselves in future courses and activities. The following list describes those courses.

- Life, Love, and Liberation surveyed African American rhetorical traditions and encouraged members to debate current and historical issues using Manning Marable and Leith Mullings's collection *Let Nobody Turn Us Around: Voices of Resistance, Reform, and Renewal.*
- Spoken Soul: Black Oral Traditions and Literacies on the ONE explored the range of black oral traditions from the folktales, work songs, spirituals and freedom songs, sermons, spoken word poetry, and Hip Hop and the blues and asked how we might use these traditions in our homes, communities, and schools not only to build awareness and pride but to improve literacy instruction for young people. This course used Daryl Cumber Dance's excellent collection *From My People: 400 Years of African American Folklore* as the central text.
- Afrofuturism: Communities, Technologies, Struggle asked people to consider how technologies can be used, reimagined, and redesigned to meet the needs of African American com-

munities and challenged people to develop futuristic visions for neighborhoods, cities, and the broader African American community. This course used articles from Alondra Nelson's special issue of *Social Text* titled *Afrofuturism* and Derrick Bell's *Afrolantica Legacies.*

- Where Do We Go From Here? Hip Hop Energy, Old School Wisdom, and a Covenant with Black America was designed specifically to suit an intergenerational audience and used Tavis Smiley's *The Covenant with Black America*, Yvonne Bynoe's *Stand and Deliver: Political Leadership, Activism, and HipHop Culture*, and Malcolm X and Martin Luther King Jr.'s classic speeches "The Ballot or the Bullet" and "Where Do We Go from Here?" to ask members to explore the power or lack of it present in Hip Hop as a movement and the lessons to be learned by this generation's activists from the civil rights and Black Power movements.
- Justice between the Dream and the Nightmare: Malcolm, Martin, and America helped us examine how both Malcolm X and Martin Luther King Jr. worked as rhetors. We also explored James Cone's argument on the importance of a synthesis of the two figures as key to reimagining black communities and understanding black history. The class used Cone's classic book on King and Malcolm X, *Malcolm, Martin, and America: A Dream or a Nightmare?*, James Washington's collection of King's speeches, *A Testament of Hope*, and George Breitmann's collection of Malcolm X speeches, *Malcolm X Speaks*, as resources. We also did this course as a yearlong course at a local high school, in conjunction with the Syracuse chapter of 100 Black Men.
- Unbought and Unbossed: Shirley Chisholm and the Challenge of Black Political Feminism used Chisholm's autobiography as our text and was part of a literacy project I designed with the director of a local nonprofit to focus on literacy as coming to public voice.
- The Organizers: Civil Rights and Black Power beyond Malcolm and Martin used Barbara Ransby's powerful work on Ella

Baker and Keith Gilyard's *Liberation Memories: The Rhetoric and Politics of John Oliver Killens* to begin to explore some of the many important voices that sometimes go unheard in histories of the movement.

- Black Politics and Participation beyond the Registration Table examined the 2008 presidential election campaign as it happened while we read Leonard Moore's work on the historic Carl Stokes election as mayor of Cleveland in 1967, *Carl B. Stokes and the Rise of Black Political Power*, and explored connections between the local and national issues surrounding the Stokes election and the Barack Obama campaign.

- "If Black English Isn't a Language, Then Tell Me What Is": Ebonics and the (Continued) Miseducation of the Black Student explored the actual features of Ebonics beyond the hype and hyperventilating that usually accompanies public conversation on this issue. Using Geneva Smitherman's *Word from the Mother*, Lisa Delpit and Teresa Perry's collection *The Real Ebonics Debate*, Keith Gilyard's *Voices of the Self*, and various folktales, poems, and movie clips, we explored ways to foster excellence for young people and adults in reading and writing while promoting an appreciation for black language in its historical and contemporary contexts.

The real story to be told about these courses is in the intellectual and practical work the course members did themselves. I got over my hesitation in asking people to write about the texts and the issues we discussed, and the results have often been amazing. The following two excerpts give just a small sample of the passion, intellect, and engagement people brought to the courses, texts, and discussions, and they show the depth of the resources that are present in these communities. They also begin to reveal the range of voices that are available when we consider our work to be that of engaging and building from the truths of those who are already present in communities. Both of the pieces challenge and encourage course members and the African American community as a whole, and the second piece, "A Village Movement" by LaToya Sawyer, became a kind of anthem for the Life, Love, and Liberation course.

My Peoples—by Ifetayo Nellons

My peoples. My peoples. Yes, my Black peoples. Stop. Stop doing nothing. Stop your lip service and be a service to the community. Whose community? The Black community. Why is it that we'll move to the suburbs and be on the neighborhood clean-up committee with a bunch of White folks, but we won't clean up the vacant lot next to our momma's house or our grand momma's house?

Why do we treat everybody else with more respect than we give ourselves? Why will we eat at a restaurant called Cracker Barrel in the middle of redneck country but we won't eat at a Black-owned restaurant on the south-side?

We need to stop trading in being Black for being successful. Let's begin deprogramming ourselves from believing the negativity about ourselves. There's nothing wrong with being Black, looking Black, acting Black, or talking Black.

You may think that no one is telling us that or that the message is not out there. But it is. Every time you turn on the television . . . the only person of color you see is in handcuffs, a mugshot, a lunatic or a fool. Except, if you watch BET or MTV, then we're all just hookers and pimps. But if you watch a channel that is more sensitive to our feelings then we're portrayed as poor crackheads who will do anything for our next fix.

We must deprogram our thinking. And not wait for anyone else to change the textbooks or television shows for us. We must do what Booker T. Washington told the south to do: "cast down your buckets where you are." We must cast down our buckets where we are. Where our heart is, where our soul is. Let us cast down our buckets in the Black community. Because we all have what we need to survive right here at our fingertips. We can do it my peoples. My Black peoples. I have faith in you.

A Village Movement—by LaToya Sawyer

This evening on the 3rd day of May 2005, we are gathered here with the knowledge that we as a people are in a state of emergency and urgency. When a locality finds itself ravaged by an outside force, usually called an act of God, be it a hurricane, tornado, earthquake, or other, and the residents are left in disarray without ample food, clothing and shelter, and the debris of the occurrence poses obstacles to their getting on with their everyday lives, sometimes threatening their very existence, a local, state or federal authority assesses the damages and declares a state of emergency.

And though I deem myself no high and mighty authority, I daily witness the evidence of such catastrophic damage in our community. I have over the course of months now studied the roots and systemic ways that the outside forces of "White America" have continued to subjugate, terrorize and decimate our people to this present date. I have also reviewed the attempts on our part and the supposed attempt on theirs to rectify this situation and have come to one resounding conclusion. The answers to our problems, the road map out of this miry maze of self-hate, deprivation, indifference and defeat can be found only in our collective past and by looking to our ancestors. However, whenever an intelligent black person opens his or her mouth to speak about black unity, without fail the seed planted so many hundred years ago rears its ugly head and says, "but we're not one monolithic people, we're too different." While this is true on one level, it should not be the end of the discussion as it often is.

In the belly of this beast called "Land of the Free," we are no more different than those who were forced into the belly of "The Good Ship Jesus" and the "Laughing Mary." Shackled together were peoples from different tribes, villages, religions, languages and other customs. But it was decided in that slave hold that in order to survive and thrive enough to overtake and kill their white captors and return to their homeland they would need to do one thing—become one village.

So for the remainder of my time, I wish to stir up within you the passion, the desire, and the necessity for a Village Movement for African peoples in America.

What does it mean to be a village? We tend to think of a village being synonymous with town or neighborhood. However, many African villages had and some still have a more definitive structure. Families lived close by and together they made up a host of elder adults, young adults, those in between and children. This by itself is not significant, but what is important is that everyone had a role and served a purpose.

Elder men may have sat in the gates sharing wisdom, elder women helped care for smaller children and passed down stories. Other adults performed tasks to keep the village functioning economically and politically and children were in training to one day do the same. Everyone under the sun was important in sustaining their community and fostering pride in their people, as well as their God. Every group of people had a belief in a creator that brought them into the world for a purpose. There were no talks of big bangs causing accidental ape families without cause or destiny. And through the changing seasons, life, both good and bad, was faced by the village together.

A woman from Ghana recently told me in reference to how her village faces struggles, she said, "we don't fight for ourselves, we fight for everyone." No one in a village need go without food, shelter, or a family's love and support.

What does this have to do with us Africans who find ourselves on the other side of the big water? We must once again institute village principles. Yes we are different persons, but let us strive together as one people! We are in a state of emergency—the war drums are crying out!

Randall Robinson says that the divide between the quality of life between blacks and whites was never meant to be bridged. But let us remember, it was never meant for us to be any other way than bent below a lash face down in a cotton field. If any one can make it and overcome, we can! We are more than conquerors!

Our error in the past has been disunity. So desperate for others to accept us as human beings, we have offered up the sacrifice of a fraction of those so called acceptable black folk to the god of "White America" in hopes that she would be pleased with us as a whole and it has failed!

Only in a village mentality, a coming together, such as this (community class), can we esteem each other properly, validate our existence and contributions and feel our true strength, shedding the layers of lies of our weakness and inferiority. Only we can help heal our wounds, so we can get ready to fight another day.

So here's the call to arms. I call all black and brown peoples in this land: men, women, boys, girls, old, young, light, dark and every shade in between, Jew, Muslim, Christian and un-decided. We need you in the village.

Part of the problem with many of our people today is they feel insignificant, looked down upon or overlooked altogether. But we won't have that, not in our village. Our strength is in those who have been marginalized by the rest of society. So here's the call to all my brothers, my sisters who think nobody wants you. After all, you've been behind bars more than not. You're not even sure you can cope out here, but you know how to thrive in there. WE NEED YOU! Who better to educate our youth on the reality and the ills of the neo-slavery prison system? And when it's time to sacrifice freedom for freedom's sake, who better than something with nothing to lose. WE NEED YOU!

My veterans we need you. When others have forgotten you, we will not. You've silenced your nightmares, flashbacks and bottled rage at unjust warfare. But don't drift away, we need you. Need you to put down the pipe, the bottle, the needles. Don't medicate that pain, that anger, use it in our struggle. Teach our young men to be warriors with a righteous anger that "ice" cannot pacify.

My "video hoes"—that is not who you are. You are beautiful women. Do not let conscienceless capitalism pervert that, because we need you.

Big Mama, we need you. I know it doesn't seem like we're listening, but keep telling your stories. Keep using those home-remedies. Swallowing Vicks ain't never hurt nobody! We need your traditions in the village.

Young girls, be young girls. Jump double-dutch, make sing-song cheers, not babies. We need your virtue and joyful laughter in the village. WE NEED YOU!

50 Cent, we need you, too, bro! We need you to stop beefin' with other brothers. There's enough respect and praise for everyone in—the village. You want us to love you like we loved Pac, but we loved Pac because he was down for us, not just money. We need you to recognize that you do owe your people 'cause you've been bought with the price of blood. 50, we need you because with all those millions of records sold you are a powerful black leader. But where are you leading? Finally dawg, since you not afraid of gunfire, we need you first in line when it's time to go to war for—the village.

We need all of you gang members to join ranks for the village ministry of defense. Represent for us, in the village.

And all my ride or die chicks, I feel you. But let's ride in the struggle. Ride for excellence in education for our children. You wanna hold somethin' down, okay, hold down a job if you need, but let's not forget to hold down our homes. Let's hold down our children, our men, and each other. You are needed in the village.

In a speech Malcolm gave after his return from Mecca, he spoke of us migrating back to Africa, but not physically, but mentally and culturally. Let's go back to the village.

In addition to the intellectual work and fellowship that local community members developed together over the course of six years' worth of Tuesday nights, the different space that we worked to create was also nurtured by the generosity of many of the scholars I listed above—James Cone, Daryl Cumber Dance, Elaine Richardson, Keith Gilyard, and Leonard Moore came to visit Syracuse to deliver lectures, hold community workshops, and break bread with us, all free of charge, simply in the spirit of building together, and Arthur Flowers, Marcelle Haddix, Kwame Dixon, and Horace Campbell

from SU all graciously did the same as a part of community symposia and visits to the Tuesday classes. Their generosity allowed us to
explore important questions and foster visions with the larger local
and campus communities.

Obviously, given my research areas, meaningful access to technologies poses some of the most important questions I believe black
communities have to engage right now, but in spite of the Afrofuturism course, the Syracuse Black Odyssey technology mini-conferenc-
es, and some of the occasional technology workshops we were able
to present, the attempt to link black rhetorical traditions, writing,
and technology in some ways represents my largest failure to date. I
say this because I have not been able to make this link a consistent
focus of inquiry every semester, despite my scholarly and pedagogical commitments. For many different reasons, I simply hadn't lined
the beats up, layered the elements in ways that worked as a regular
part of every course. This failure has pushed me over the last couple
of years to develop a detailed curriculum based on the digital griot
that, while developed for a community audience, I can use, revise,
and sample in many different community and campus contexts. The
best short summary I can use to describe my pedagogical commitments at the intersection of writing and technologies is that from my
first efforts at volunteering in a computer lab at Cleveland's Hough
neighborhood in the mid-1990s to the present, I've always been clear
that technology in/with/and writing means far more than simply
creating documents with iMovie or Photoshop or FinalCut, more
than mashups or blogs or wikis or Facebook profiles, more than the
newest shiny objects or most advanced software or sense of the cool
to be found in geek culture. Given the commitments I've layered
throughout this chapter, my goals in developing such a course are to

- practice and present writing as a multimodal, rhetorically based
  set of skills and abilities in which black people see their linguistic and discursive practices as central and celebrated and see
  oral, print, and digital literacies as inextricably linked;
- promote a critical awareness of digital writing technologies and
  a comfort level using them, examining technologies' potentials,
  problems, and ways they present possibilities for democratic

action and implication in unjust systems of power, privilege, and exploitation;

- present technology issues as subjects for humanistic inquiry rather than as merely writing spaces or sets of skills one needs in order to "succeed"—to continually examine African American relationships on macro- and micro- levels or, as my colleague Collin Brooke argues in his book *Lingua Franca*, to examine engagements with technologies on the levels of code, practice, and culture, simultaneously;
- examine black rhetorical and storytelling traditions as presenting a deep democratic alternative historiography that builds from the truths, tropes, and experiences of a people who are still not present enough in higher education and other so-called mainstream American institutions—and an alternative historiography that offers important perspectives on what it means to be human in relationship with technologies and technological systems;
- encourage an ethos of both participation in technologies, education systems, and the larger society on one's own terms and resistance to orders of domination;
- challenge writers to see themselves as archivists, "real-life documentarians" (shoutout to Mos Def and Talib Kweli), and reinterpreters, remixers of traditions, as opposed to simply looking to make a point, develop an argument, or defend and develop a thesis, using technologies to tell and preserve their own stories, to become their own archivists and canon-makers like Papa LaBas and the best DJs;
- build community by using the writing, sharing, and dissemination of stories that participants tell, write, and collect.

I see this as a yearlong course, combining a seminar/cipher approach with a workshop, in order to link the local community and the campus and critical thinking/discussion with hands-on experience in digital environments. I have used all of the readings and activities listed here in various parts of my teaching and community work but not yet in the space of a single community course. The sample course I present here would continue to follow the Tuesday night format that we established for the other community courses, using that session for storytelling, discussion, and readings while adding a Saturday afternoon "studio" session in our computer lab on campus that would combine storytelling, writing activities, and demos of various digital tools. In addition to the computer lab (a Mac lab on our campus), we would also use cameras and voice recorders.

Listed below are some of the readings I would use in such a course and have used in other courses (many of which have been cited throughout this book) and short descriptions of some of the activities.

READINGS

Books

Abdul Alkalimat, *The African American Experience in Cyberspace*

Derrick Bell, *Afrolantica Legacies*

Katie Cannon, introduction and conclusion to *Katie's Canon: Womanism and the Soul of the Black Community*

Jeff "Chairman" Mao with Afrika Bambaataa, "You Spin Me Round (Like a Record, Baby)," in *Vibe History of Hip Hop*

Harold Courlander, *A Treasury of African American Folklore* (selections)

Daryl Cumber Dance, ed., *From My People: 400 Years of African American Folklore* (selections)

Linda Goss, ed., *Talk That Talk: An Anthology of African American Storytelling* (selections)

Alondra Nelson, "Future Texts," in *Afrofuturism: A Special Edition of Social Text*, ed. Alondra Nelson

Alondra Nelson, ed., *Technicolor: Race, Technology, and Everyday Life* (selections)

Cynthia Selfe and Gail Hawisher, *Literate Lives in the Information Age: Narratives of Literacy from the United States* (selections)

Bruce Sinclair, "Integrating the Histories of Race and Technology," in *Technology and the African American Experience: Needs and Opportunities for Study*

Geneva Smitherman, *Word from the Mother: Language and African Americans* (selections including chapter 1, "African American Language: So Good It's Bad," and chapter 4, "Honeyz and Playaz Talkin That Talk")

Folktales

"Signifyin Monkey" (including Oscar Brown's version)
"Shine"
"Shine and the *Titanic*"
"Stagger Lee"
"Dolemite"
"The Distribution of the Orishas' Powers"
"Why Obatala Trembles at the River"
"Br'er Rabbit and the Briar Patch"
"King of de World" (by Zora Neale Hurston)
"Why Anansi Hides in Corners, a Tale from Ghana"
"Anancy an Him Story, a Tale from Jamaica"
"Spread the Word: A Storyteller's Rap" (by Linda Goss)

Speeches and Essays

James Baldwin, "The Creative Process"
Combahee River Collective statement
Angela Davis, "I Am a Revolutionary Black Woman"
Martin Luther King Jr., "Remaining Awake through a Great Revolution"
Malcolm X, "Message from the Grassroots" and "The Ballot or the Bullet"
David Walker, selections from "Appeal"

ACTIVITIES

1. Intro Session—Autobiography and/or Technology Literacy Narrative. In this intro session, I've used YouTube clips to have people introduce themselves or sometimes one of their peers after some paired conversation. After that, I would sometimes ask people to write a short piece describing the soundtrack they would use to tell some part of their life story or to describe their experiences with literacy, education, and/or technology. This would set up more formal technology literacy narratives based on the idea of cultural ecologies of literacy that Cynthia Selfe and Gail Hawisher develop.

2. Black Oral Traditions from Shine to Shine. Just a quick example here: sometimes we would read the classic tale "Shine and the

Titanic," both for fun and as critique of Western worship of science and technology. To show the connections and consistencies in the tradition, I would then play either songs from Hip Hop artist Shine or Steve Harvey's remix/retelling of the Shine story in *The Original Kings of Comedy.*

3. Storytelling Festival. This activity is designed not only to introduce people to the wide range of stories in the tradition but to work the idea that one can develop his or her own writing voice and/or personae (in print or digital spaces) by developing his or her own way of telling a story.

4. Two Turntables and a Mouse: Beat-making, Beat-matching, and the Art of the Mix. I have not fully explored these ideas yet, but I want to have actual DJs co-teaching with me, where participants will have a chance to create their own beats by layering various samples and other elements and learn to blend one song into another, the way a DJ would at a party or on a mixtape, as a way of teaching writers to attend more closely to how they set transitions between ideas and sources in a text. I also want to use this activity to explore the tensions in copyright debates by doing versions where participants can use anything from any source and then versions where they can use elements only that they can get clearance for, whether based on fair use arguments or Creative Commons licensing.

5. This Is the Remix: Digital (Re)tellings of Black Folktales. In one version of this activity, I ask participants to use images, sounds, and anything else they want to tell their own version of a favorite folktale. They key here is that I ask people not to use the actual text of the story but rather to experiment with selection and arrangement of other materials to create their narrative, their version.

6. Oral History Project/iMovie/Slideshow. Given Syracuse's particular context, this project would be connected to gathering oral histories of the "Fifteenth Ward," a section of town that was decimated by the construction of Interstate 81, along with the ways that residents with personal, family, or cultural ties to this neighborhood imagine its redevelopment given the ironic turn that politicians are now considering tearing down the portion of the interstate that dislocated so many people.

7. Technology Transformation Project. This is an activity that I have used in classes occasionally since I was a graduate student at Penn State. Using Ben Chappell's "Take a Little Ride with Me: Lowriding and the Poetics of Scale," we examine lowrider culture and the way it is transforming automotive technology and see how it reflects both one's individual personality and identity as well as his or her cultural identity. I then ask class participants to imagine such a reworking of the computer—from the code to the case, from programming to aesthetics—to include their vision of what a computer might do, might look like, if it were grounded in their own cultural perspectives and their own individual personalities.

8. Individual Blog. Participants write on some issue related to preserving folktales or other black oral traditions in the United States or in the diaspora.

9. Spoken Word Poetry/Speeches/Spitboxing with Voice Recorders. Such demonstrations can be uploaded to a personal Web site or YouTube.

10. The Intellectual Mixtape. Here we would return to the beginning, but rather than use the mixtape as a soundtrack to either a memoir or literacy narrative, I would ask people to create a mix CD that serves as their soundtrack to the ideas, readings, and activities of the course. I would ask the participants to compile and arrange songs that reflect not only the course's content but also their reactions, interpretations, interrogations, and feedback (thus inviting not only reflexive praxis but even some of that siggin, Flava Flavin that Carmen Kynard's students enacted on Blackboard and is an important part of the co-construction of knowledge that Moss describes).

As I've described throughout this book, the point of a project like this is to encourage participants to see themselves as griots, to value the oral tradition and print and digital literacies, and to develop writing and rhetorical practices that link the three toward the goals of building community and deep democracy through critical literacy.

By presenting a bit of history of our work in Syracuse and a vision for scholarship through the lens of the digital griot as I apply

Moss, Marable, and others to the DJ's practice of the mix, I am obviously offering only one possible mix out of many valuable ones. This particular layering of beats, voices, harmonies, and tensions that faded into and out of many different texts is one that attempts to take a realistic view of the scholar's work and to make space for those pursuing community work who cannot—or do not want to— feel pressure to separate themselves from the struggles, joys, pains, beauty, visions, and discursive practices of those he or she hopes to serve. The digital griot as one model among many offers a unified view of oral performance, print literacy, and digital technologies grounded in the specific oral traditions of African Americans, even as it engages print and digital literacies. No mix is perfect, and no mix is ever guaranteed to work, but the mix as a set of rhetorical practices that asks rhetors to value layering, balance, transition, tim- ing, priority, proportion, and selection can allow a synchronizing of multiple discourses and a synthesizing of difficult binaries even as it allows a place to stand within those discourses and binaries, no matter how temporary such a stance might ultimately be.

Shoutout: The Hiphop Archive (www.hiphoparchive.org)

This digital griot project, created and maintained by Marcyliena Morgan, makes real Tricia Rose's imperative to pursue flow, layering, and rupture by collecting, preserving, explicating, and disseminating Hip Hop lyrics and culture toward the ends of developing scholars and scholarship on Hip Hop, building community, and pursuing activism for social and racial justice. The archive hosts Hip Hop University, a space that includes bibliographies, standards for schol- arship, courses, events, conferences, and listings of underground radio outlets that counter stereotypical notions of Hip Hop. The site includes a blog connecting Hip Hop to political and cultural affairs, an Introduction to Hip Hop section, and a searchable ar- chive of lyrics from throughout Hip Hop's history. Morgan's work on the site and that of the large number of volunteers and advisory board members who help to maintain it is about the creation and preservation of knowledge as well as the creation and preservation of community, directly linking members of various generations, ideologies, and social positions in that work.

3

Remix: Afrofuturistic Roadmaps—
Rememory Remixed for a Digital Age

IN SOME WAYS, this chapter could seem to be an exercise in redundancy. Generational gaps make up one of the oldest stories in the world: every culture has them; every era has them. Many movements are partially created out of the sense that a new generation has arrived on the scene with a new vision and a new direction. Within African American literature, the Harlem Renaissance and the Black Arts Movement contained an explicit generational exigence, and in the current moment, Tony Medina, Samiya A. Bashir, and Quraysh Ali Lansana defined their 2002 anthology *Role Call* as a generational anthology marking the presence of yet another crew of young lions, or, as they put it, writers who were under forty at the time of the anthology's publication. Many activists, writers, and scholars quote Frantz Fanon's imperative from *The Wretched of the Earth*: "Every generation must, out of relative obscurity, find its mission, fulfill it, or betray it" (145). So this chapter begins to tell, yet again, one of the oldest stories in the world, because I believe that one of the most intriguing—and for many, most frustrating—challenges in African American rhetoric today has to do with the contemporary manifestations of that old, old story.

In this case, the story involves generational splits that exist between those who have lived through the civil rights and Black Power movements and those youth and young adults who have no living memory of this particular era. The tensions between these two groups foster sharp debates and, even worse, silence as young people and elders often talk *about* each other and about that chasm but rarely *to* each other. In this chapter, I want to explore the ways these generational tensions are encoded in what I am calling the "back in the day" narrative and the rhetorical functions of such narratives. I argue here that this form, with the cultural nostalgia that marks its use, has become a central element of the everyday rhetorical performances of African Americans from the early 1990s onward. During this period, the "back in the day" narrative became far more than a loose collection of tales—these tales became crystallized into an "old school" ethos that is about much more than the continual tensions every generation has with the previous or next generation in every cultural group. Rather than merely the usual grousing young people and elders subject each other to, the "back in the day" narrative and the old school ethos it signals reflect deeply rooted anxieties about black culture, identity, and activism in a digital age. Given the very real issues African Americans continue to face, addressing these generational tensions—in other words, finding ways to get elders and young people communicating with each other and finding collective answers to these issues—is one of the key rhetorical challenges of our time. Because it is such a key challenge, I also want to explore ways that young people and elders might communicate across this chasm and the serious debates that lie within it.

The "back in the day" narrative not only is a form that reflects generational tensions and a community's anxieties about a difficult age but also is a form that represents powerful collective memory at work that helps point the way forward into that new age. The everyday griots who use this form engage in a remix of rememory, identifying specific values that can help preserve community in the midst of social rupture. After analyzing the rhetorical functions of the "back in the day" narrative as a living remix, I want to suggest that the genre of the DJ's remix—and one particular version of it, the "old school/new school" remix—offers a conceptual metaphor for the kinds of textual and technological syntheses that can bridge old school and new school and print, oral, and digital literacies in an Afrofuturistic approach to activism and rhetorical performance.

The remix is a common, if somewhat floating, signifier among compositionists. It is usually meant as any reuse of an original text, as a repurposing of that text, or sometimes as any recombination of elements from many sources in the creation of a new text of any kind. These conceptions are much closer to how DJs mean and use the mix than how I am using remix here. The remix as employed by these scholars is prized as a concept because of how it values a sense of play with texts and various nontextual elements and because it allows teachers and students generic possibilities beyond those immediately rooted in the standard academic essay. It is also valued because of its semantic proximity to postmodern notions of pastiche and because it gives teachers a concept of revision that their students can easily grasp, thanks to its ubiquity in popular culture. Johndan Johnson-Eilola and Stuart Selber explain its appeal in those terms while also noting the possibilities inherent in the remix for incorporating many different kinds of materials (images, text, recorded voices, video). They also contend that the remix helps trouble the theoretical waters of "originality" as the main or only value in student writing and point toward greater appreciation for arrangement.

Catherine Latterell's reader/textbook *Remix: Reading and Composing Culture* is grounded in a similar theoretical approach, arguing like Johnson-Eilola and Selber that the remix defines the culture students live and write in. Her text picks up on the idea that students now are prosumers—both consuming and creating content as an important part of their lives. On Latterell's professional Web site and in text that is used frequently to promote the book, she defines remix culture as a "do it yourself, collaborative, and creative culture in which they are the writers, designers, and creators." Like Stephanie Vie in her article "Digital Divide 2.0," Latterell believes that our job in the classroom is to get students to critically examine the technologies they often use without careful consideration of the assumptions behind the tools and spaces and the complex issues of identity and community that surround them. She also is attracted to the concept because it allows students ways of juxtaposing texts and ideas from academic and popular culture as well as other forms of public discourse and encourages students to create a wide range of print, oral, and digital texts.

Kathleen Blake Yancey mines the conceptual possibilities in the remix even further, identifying the remix as an idea that has methodological implications for scholarship in composition and asserting that a view of the remix can lead to a reshaping of graduate curricula in order to make them more relevant to a constantly changing writing and technology landscape. Her article "Redesigning Graduate Education in Composition and Rhetoric: The Use of Remix as Concept, Material, and Method" argues that the concept is far more than metaphor and allows comp/rhet an opportunity to address the clunky and cumbersome processes of curricular change that Alex Reid (discussed in chapter 1) wrestles with in his work, implementing tools like iTunes University.

Based simply on my experience of growing up and coming of age in the 1980s, I personally always took the "remix" to be the creation of a new version of a song or text, a remake undertaken to fit a different context, purpose, or audience, where the "re" in the mix might involve rearranging elements, changing the beat (as in the case of a dance remix), extending the original (as in the case of a radio version being remixed as an Extended Play—EP or 12", for those who grew up with vinyl), and/or edits to the language to make edgier songs more palatable for radio play or more funky and more irreverent for audiences who didn't like the sanitized radio edit. A remixed text might use different samples, slightly or significantly different melodies or beats, additional or removed voices, and layerings of all of the above. The point for me, from my first job as an eleven-year-old sweeping up and taking out the garbage at Price-Rite, a record store in my Wade Park neighborhood in Cleveland, until I entered comp/rhet as a discipline, was that the remix was a thorough revision of a song or text that could stand on its own as a separate text, even as it was rooted in an identifiable original. Cue up Henry Louis Gates's definition of signifying as repetition with a key difference (via Geneva Smitherman's more layered description of siggin in the 1977 classic *Talkin and Testifyin*, where she discusses at length the competitive, trumping impulse involved in the practice).

The most useful definition of the remix, though, for the purposes of this chapter comes not from my own reminiscences of local Cleveland record stores, radio, college parties, or nightclubs but from Eduardo Navas on the blog Remix Theory. Navas's definition squares well with that already used or implied by many in composition. He offers a general definition of remix as "the global activity of the creative and efficient exchange of information made possible by digital technologies that is supported by the practice of cut/copy and paste." After clarifying that this history began with the Jamaican form of the "dub version" that Kool Herc and Afrika Bambaataa transformed in the Bronx through the breakbeat and continued throughout the 1970s as Hip Hop and disco extended its theoretical and practical possibilities, Navas pushes this general definition and history further, however, to offer a specific articulation: the remix is "a reinterpretation of a pre-existing song, meaning that the 'aura' of the original will be dominant in the remixed version." He also offers a taxonomy of three specific types of remixes: (1) an extended version, which grows most directly from the Jamaican dub; (2) a selective version, which might choose to delete some elements of the original and add new sounds or elements while "keeping the essence of the song intact"; and (3) a reflexive remix, one that "allegorizes and extends the aesthetic of sampling, where the remixed version challenges the aura of the original, and claims autonomy, even when it carries the name of the original; material is added or deleted, but the original tracks are largely left intact to be recognizable." In this third case, Navas cites the Mad Professor's album *No Protection* as a text that stands on its own, even as it is "completely dependent" on Massive Attack's original *Protectioni.*

The point of the remix as a valuable concept for me, beyond the rich ways in which composition has taken it up, is not merely in the processes of copy/paste or in encouraging new arrangements of widely varying oral, print, and digital materials in the writing classroom, though these possibilities are clearly important to me. The real theoretical possibilities of the remix lie in all three of Navas's versions—the remix as dub version, selective rearrangement, and critical reflective gesture producing the paradox of independent yet dependent texts. This is what makes the remix Papa LaBas's and Alondra Nelson's *future text*: the fact that it allows an explicit linking of "old school" and "new school," a synchronizing of generational commonalities and tensions that allows, even demands, innovation while remaining linked with histories and traditions. The sample as a form allows this same kind of synchronizing (many people already know that the songs of James Brown and Parliament-Funkadelic are still the most sampled in all of the following generation's Hip Hop), but the remix hits the blend differently. It maintains more focus on the original text and demands a coherent response, an overall plan to the re-visioned text. Longtime radio personality Tom Joyner made the old school/new school remix a staple of his morning radio shows for exactly this synchronizing purpose. By playing remixes he commissioned from well-known DJ Steve "Silk" Hurley, Joyner intentionally linked younger generations to their elders in the same groove, allowing for conceptions of unities among and across these groups even as the generational differences were still audible.

The need for this kind of synchronizing of generational texts, narratives, goals, and strategies has long been a pressing one in African American communities and among black activists and, I argue, an important one in framing the study of African American rhetoric. The "back in the day" narrative demonstrates exactly why African American rhetoric as an area of study is in such need of this kind of synchronizing as it foregrounds these generational tensions and at the same time shows the possibilities for a remix that provides a new narrative and a new roadmap into the future.

I have long thought in general, casual ways about these stories and the ways they function in African American culture, but two separate though related moments came together within a week of each other to let me know something more is at work, that there is something different, something a little more pronounced in the internal tensions among blackfolk at this particular time. At the 2007 State of Black America forum, tensions over culture, history, and identity exploded in a debate between Eddie Glaude and Al Sharpton. In this encounter that is known more for his having called Al Sharpton and Jesse Jackson "hustlers" than for the specific argument he makes, Glaude challenged the conventional wisdom that young people are somehow less committed, less grounded in their history and all about "the bling" and at the same time challenged elders, saying, "I cannot stomach when people use history to beat up on young folk." Part of

Glaude's argument is that we must have a different approach to history, where we somehow make it real for young people so that they have a living connection to those events and people and forms of knowledge. Another part of the argument is that the very elements of popular culture that are used to attack young people were a part of every other era in black culture, from the soul of Marvin Gaye back to the blues and before. The stakes of our refusing to recognize the links between eras and continuing to buy into hype that youth today are somehow more degraded, less committed to struggle, less willing to learn, and only focused on money and sex are high for Glaude. The result will be even greater division in black communities because, in his opinion, young people will then have little regard for the history that elders say they must know if they hear it or see it only in ways that minimize them. As important as history is to us all, the greatness of that history for Glaude is that it has led African Americans to a moment we have never seen before, with complexities, difficulties, and possibilities that history alone cannot lead us through. Sharpton's response was interesting in that he maintained his position that young people have fallen short of their obligations to the community and each other and that we must continue to challenge each other to do more, but he avoided or dismissed the substance of Glaude's challenge. He also maintained the attitude that things are seriously wrong with young people and youth culture. This particular debate shows not only the generational fault line but also just how much that fault line has moved and is moving.

Within a week of the 2007 State of Black America gathering, the other moment happened: Katie Cannon captured these same tensions succinctly, and in far more nuanced ways, without resorting to the kind of cultural nostalgia that leads some elders to believe they lived in and forged some kind of golden age and without the anger that rises to the surface of the Glaude/Sharpton clip. I traveled to Richmond to interview her for a project on Black Theology (having no idea that it would come to be such a contested movement and caught up in so much public discussion during the 2008 presidential campaign), asking her to assess the history, to talk about the future of Black Theology and womanist theology and to describe her own work in those movements. Her first comment surprised me. When I asked her to take stock of these movements, the successes, challenges, possibilities, and needs for future work, she opened the interview by saying, "I don't know how to talk to these younger scholars who identify themselves as postmodern, postfeminist, as if we've already come through the struggle." She told me that her major challenge as a preacher and theologian—and the major challenge for elder womanist and black theologians—is the search for language and strategies to cross that chasm, to live and work along that fault line.

It is my contention that these generational tensions and frustrations become encoded in the form of the "back in the day" narrative and that this narrative has become a central one in all kinds of African American rhetorical performances. I use the phrase "'back in the day' narrative" to identify a genre of reflections and stories that refer to an important time in the past that lies within living memory. Thus, these tales are fit in a different category from reflections on other historical periods and are also different from those tales that are referred to as etiological tales—tales about the beginnings of a culture, nation, or people. The major themes of the "back in the day" narrative—that we must do a far better job in passing on the history, knowledge, and traditions of our past to our young people; the idea that we have somehow lost something significant even as so many other things have changed for the better—also emerge in film and literature. Some movies, like the Hip Hop love story *Brown Sugar*, are based completely on renderings of this narrative form and its implication that we have lost something important along the way to the current moment. Others, like *Love Jones*, have it implied in the representations of many of the main characters. Darius Lovehall, one of the film's protagonists, types his work out on a typewriter rather than a computer, rides an older motorcycle, and listens to jazz standards like Duke Ellington and John Coltrane's "In a Sentimental Mood," all of which mark him as an old soul, a "throwback" kind of character, while several other characters present themselves visually in thrift store chic in critique of the incessant consumerism and global capitalism that seem to be hallmarks of contemporary culture. "Spoken Word" poetry as a genre, as a movement that gained popularity in African American communities in the 1990s, depended on this same old school/old soul argument, emerging as it did as with similar critiques of Hip Hop and pop culture's excesses. Interestingly, this pocket of popular culture shows us a moment of youth culture exhibiting the very qualities many elders claim young people have lost—particularly in its resistance to and critique of materialism and consumerism and its longing for deep connections with African American history, culture, and the elders in a sense of collective struggle. These film manifestations of the "back in the day" narrative begin to show that this form is not merely about elders fussing out the youngins but about a broader set of both contentions and commonplaces within black communities.

Poet Kamau Daáood offers a literary treatment and a compelling version of this longing and sense of loss in his poem "Blakey's Sticks." In this poem, he renders jazz drummer Art Blakey's drumsticks as symbol, as metaphor for the wisdom of the elders desperately needed by a generation that has, for him, lost its way:

> These children of asphalt, blinded by grey and neon
> Tonguetied with empty money clips
> Looking for the faint footprints of home training,
> Deaf to the voice of the old ones.

Our current moment is one that continues to dehumanize and de-sensitize black people and one that poses challenges that our youth are unprepared for:

> a spider, waiting for you on the world wide web,
> wants you to pick cotton in cyberspace
> wants you to wear a bowtie of yellow police tape
> wants you to snort the white lines of chalk on asphalt
> through a didgeridoo.

Frustrated like many others with the seeming individualism and money-at-all-costs attitude of young people, Daáood calls them "children of asphalt" who not only are not prepared with the armor they need to protect them but are oblivious to or stubbornly dismissive of the need for any such protection, as they "refuse to wear the psychic beehive hat, swarm of conceptual killerbees awaiting you at dawn. Here, where I is the first and only letter in the alphabet." To his credit, Daáood in this poem is critical of the entire culture, not just young people, but his reading of this generation of youth is that they are so absorbed with what the society seems to offer that they have turned away from traditions and therefore their own people. His poem deserves a far more detailed reading than I offer here, because it is a very nuanced and beautiful piece that calls us all to lower ourselves more deeply into the knowledge to be gained not from blind adherence to tradition but in a searching of the eyes, actions, and knowledge of those "souls aged in struggle . . . doers, builders."

Beyond the public dimensions of this fault line as it is manifested in literature, speeches, and films, discussions of generational tensions in this African American cultural moment are a prominent part of everyday rhetorical performances in black communities. A striking example of the centrality of this issue and the role of the "back in the day" narrative as a genre in need of exploration occurred when one of the African American student groups on campus invited me to attend a meeting. The group had dedicated one of their general body meetings to examining these tensions, titling the evening's session "Candy Girl vs. Crank That Soulja Boy." I immediately felt old and out of place because New Edition's 1983 "Candy Girl" is the last song I would have picked to represent the "old school" and saw the move as particularly ironic given New Edition's entry into R/B as a bubblegum group—that is, not exactly what the oldheads yearn for when they talk about "real music." I went, partially because of these intriguing ironies but also because I was glad to see the group thinking through these issues, and I wondered what their take would be.

The evening session began with the group's president inviting discussion with such prompts as "Tell me about a childhood memory," "Tell me about a story your parents used to tell you back in the day," "Tell me about a song you grew up with that marks an important time in your life." These prompts elicited the requested information with some of the to-be-expected laughter at the old folks' expense because of the nature of their stories—insert your own joke here about walking to school fifteen miles one way in the snow while living in some remote, tiny town. One of the many reasons this gathering on this night was fascinating to me was because these eighteen- to twenty-year-olds unanimously flipped the script and spent nearly an hour reveling in their own "back in the day" narratives, talking energetically about how things are so different for young children growing up now than they were for them when they came up. They cited countless examples of how rigorously they were disciplined, of the strong communal elements to their neighborhoods, of the utter declension in the music between when they were growing up in the 1990s and today, these kids "three years old and already knowing how to do the Soulja Boy [dance] or singing about how their lip gloss is popping," to paraphrase one of the participants. Never mind that these same students were likely to be found doing the Soulja Boy and singing about their own lip gloss—they were already beginning to appropriate the role and voice of elders wondering what happened to society. So a group meeting that I read as intended to spark dialogue about how grownfolk and elders have maligned *them* as being apathetic or unengaged or unaware of the struggle turned into one where they were creating the exact same stories, mildly remixed for their moment. This meeting and this moment became one of the hints to me that there is far more than generational tension encoded into the "back in the day" narrative. I'll develop this point more in a moment, but let me offer a few of my favorite "back in the day" narratives:

Back when I was comin up, you had discipline. If I got caught doing something wrong, Ms. So-and-So would whup my behind right then and there, and then I would always get another whuppin when I got home, because the news *always* beat you home—even if you didn't have a phone.

Man, you remember having to go out and get your own switch? I couldn't stand that! You would go out there trying to take your time, trying to stall, and you had better not bring back no skinny switch, either! That would just make it worse.

Back in the day, gospel music was about God. I'm tired of all this Hip Hop in gospel. Some people are goin to hell for all of that. Gospel was gospel back in the day. Give me some James Cleveland and some Aretha Franklin and some Edwin Hawkins over this nonsense anytime.

Kids don't even know how to go outside and play these days, just sitting in the house playing video games and watching TV all the time. We used to have to make our own fun. You had to have imagination back in the day.

We used to be more united back in the day. Everybody was struggling, but we all shared what we had.

Back in the day there wasn't no "time out"—if you acted up, you got knocked the hell out.

People used to spend more time outside back in the day. We used to sit on our porches, go out to the park, barbecue together just because—not even having a reason.

The neighborhoods were safer. We didn't even have to lock our doors at night. We would keep the main door open and just close the screen door.

Back in the day, before blackfolk got to chasing others out into the suburbs and before "urban renewal," we used to all live together. Young people could be in the hood and still see doctors, grocers, teachers, and pastors. Now they have no way of seeing their own people as successes in their own neighborhoods.

Back in the day there wasn't all of this nonsense with guns. A fight didn't mean you were risking your life because somebody would go get their boys or pull out a piece [gun]. People used to knuckle up and fight, and half the time they would get along the next time they saw each other.

Since the early 1990s, these narratives have become more than collective storytelling, however, to take on a central role in the everyday rhetoric of African American culture. There has been a shift from the mere presence or importance of these narratives to their congealing into what I am calling an old school ethos. This old school ethos is marked by the shift to centralize these narratives in the public discourse of our current cultural moment. Beginning in the early 1990s, in a moment contemporaneous with what many believe was a major shift in African American popular culture, and an especially pronounced shift in Hip Hop as a manifestation of that culture, these narratives became encoded in Hip Hop, standup comedy, speeches, sermons, and many other texts as a set of values that was deployed to develop standing or credibility with black audiences. Instead of just looking back to the old school, people *became* old school and wore it as a badge of pride. These tales about how much better things were back in the day took on even greater importance as signs that during the 1960s, 1970s, and 1980s, African American communities were more closely connected because of bonds forged in collective struggle and also because the ravages of deindustrialization, global capitalism, automation, class flight into suburbs and exurbs, the rise of computers and the digital information age, HIV/ AIDS, crack cocaine, and other concerns had not yet torn black communities asunder—or at least the effects of such ruptures were not as clear to those looking back. This is one reason why standup comedy over the last two decades has been so full of jokes about Kool-Aid and the little TV on top of the big TV and having to actually get up to change the channel. In Toni Morrison's *Beloved*, rememory or remembering to remember is essential because the past carries unspeakable acts, untold horrors. In the remix of rememory encoded into the "back in the day" narrative, the unspeakable acts and untold horrors live in the present, as black communities witness devastation around them with little opportunity to tell the truths of that devastation within a larger national narrative of great progress.

One example of how these narratives became crystallized and employed as a kind of ethos comes from Steve Harvey's routine as he prepares to introduce Cedric the Entertainer in the 2000 comedy tour and movie *The Original Kings of Comedy*. All of the comics affirm that they are old school, and in this clip Harvey says, "I'm old school," and later he says, "If you don't get into old school, you done missed it. See, I'm a '74 bruh. Cleveland, Ohio, Glenville High School 1974. When music was music." At another point in the routine, he says, "I ain't convertin'," and then uses several old school songs from artists like Earth, Wind & Fire, the Ohio Players, and Lenny Williams to bring the audience together in a feel-good sing-along anthem moment and announces that for anyone who isn't "feelin'" him in his reminiscing, that's just too bad. In the routine, Harvey develops the point about his being old school with many themes, often contrasting old school music to Hip Hop, with one of the most important differences being that old school artists sang about love. The argument, by extension, is that blackfolk were more willing to express love to and for each other. Along with his own use of this material to frame the entire tour, the rapturous response of the audience shows viewers that his move worked—that the old school is not just a tactic to develop his own credibility and good-will but that it serves as the basis for a collective ethos that is just as much about building consensus in the current moment as it ever was about the past. All of this reclaiming of the old school is a marked difference from African American popular culture in the 1970s and 1980s, even into 1986 when Run DMC declared in their song "King of Rock" that they were brand new and would never, ever be old school. Whether these narratives and their tellers are right about their explicit and implied arguments about an African American golden age in the civil rights and Black Power era and whether we have somehow fallen away from those values and commitments in our current digital age is not my concern here. Rather than focus on the content of these long-standing debates, my interest is in the function of these narratives that undergird everyday African American rhetorical practice.

There are many points to be made about these narratives and how they function. For example, they are consistent across the Saturday night/Sunday morning continuum in African American culture. Church folk tell them; Hip Hop fans tell them. As I noted earlier, they are consistent among many different age groups—youth, young adults, and elders claim a stake in how we forge histories and in how we see the present through creating, using, telling, and signifyin on these tales. My larger point here is that the "back in the day" narrative is not nearly as much about "back in the day" as it might seem. Even when the tone is oppositional—in other words, contrasting past moments with our contemporary moment with the intent of critiquing either young people or the broader culture—this form, this genre, is about right now. The "back in the day" narrative works as a trope for resistance, reform, and renewal, to borrow Manning Marable and Leith Mullings's phrase from the subtitle of their anthology *Let Nobody Turn Us Around*, by fulfilling the following functions:

- affirming black humanity by recognizing something special in black culture (special knowledge, experiences, consciousness)
- forging a collective memory, or acting as a form of what Toni Morrison calls "rememory"—the active, aching need to work at remembering that which is often threatened, stolen, or lost
- serving as a touchstone in developing African American cultural commonplaces—common values, knowledge, outlooks— and thus as a tool for developing the very unity people often see lacking in the present moment
- making the argument for those values, that knowledge, or that outlook as the basis for a collective agenda for the future

To put these four points differently, an important function of the "back in the day" narrative and the old school ethos it contributes to in African American culture is to remix history in order to point a new way forward. Before notions of being old school came to be commodified in mainstream news and entertainment television shows and "throwback" sneakers, jerseys, and other items, this narrative form worked, and still works, to recapture the ideas and values of the civil rights and Black Power eras and even to bridge those very different ideologies in this moment as a roadmap for a different kind of consciousness now and an Afrofuturistic roadmap for the action in the future. Let me take one of the narratives above and attempt to offer some evidence for my claims here. One of the staples of this genre is that African Americans were more unified back in the day, and because of the thousands and thousands of people involved in the mass movements of the 1950s and 1960s and the many organizations that were involved in the struggles for racial justice, those stories have particular resonance with many people. However, anyone who studies African American rhetoric or history in any depth would never allow the claim that blackfolk were automatically more unified in any one era to go unchecked. As a matter of fact, if there is any one thing African Americans were unified about, it was the need for more unity in the ongoing struggle. David Walker, Ida B. Wells Barnett, W. E. B. Du Bois, Ella Baker, Amy Jacques Garvey and Marcus Garvey, Audre Lorde, Malcolm, Martin, Claudia Jones, and many, many more, across sharp ideological divisions and across eras, all issued some kind of call for greater unity, either among the masses of black people or among particular groups within. Another example rests with the popular tales of how we did a better job of disciplining our children back in the day. Really? We did? That's why *Cooley High*, a coming-of-age film released in 1975 and set in 1964 taking up the ills of the education scene in black America, feels so much like 1989's *Lean on Me* to me. Michael Eric Dyson makes this very point in his essay "We Never Were What We Used to Be: The Politics of Black Nostalgia," namely that our nostalgia is often a rewriting of history—a remix that often judges the contemporary moment and young people in particular as having fallen short of some imagined golden age.

So if people were not more disciplined or more unified or more committed to each other or less materialistic during this time—or if we were not universally so—what else is at work in this creation of a communal ethos, or mythos? What do we make of the fact that many different generations employ these narratives toward very similar purposes? Even when it seems to be the case, the real rhetorical function of the "back in the day" narrative is not to attack young people, and it is not really about the creation of a golden age in the past. The "back in the day" narrative is an intentional remixing of history, undertaken in the attempt to create a common interpretation of the past, to enable arguments about how to move forward through the ruptures and dislocations that mark the current moment and to set an agenda for future action. To put it another way, the "back in the day" narrative is actually an example of Alondra Nelson's future text, an Afrofuturistic rhetorical gesture and genre. Nelson and several others who developed Afrofuturism as a concept in the mid-1990s used it to begin to ask and answer questions of how African Americans might address questions of identity and activism in a digital age. In her search for an archetype for engaging questions about African American relationships to technologies that moved beyond the utopian/dystopian polemic present in many technology narratives, Nelson based her concept of Afrofuturism on the necromancy of Ishmael Reed's HooDoo protagonist Papa LaBas in *Mumbo Jumbo* and his combination of futuristic vision and commitment to grounding that vision in a deep, searching knowledge of the past. This combination and the committed, constant search that undergirds it helps to create conditions where

> the next generation will be successful in creating a text that can codify Black culture: past, present, and future. Rather than a "Western" image of the future that is increasingly detached from the past, or equally problematic, a future-primitive perspective that fantasizes an uncomplicated return to ancient culture, LaBas foresees the distillation of African diasporic experience, rooted in the past but not weighed down by it, contiguous yet continually transformed. (Nelson 8)

To put it another way, Nelson's argument, as I note in chapter 1 and intentionally sample and reuse here, is that African American culture is in desperate need of "synchronizing," or synthesizing, past and future. The "back in the day" narrative is a first step in this kind of synchronizing, where black people are asking themselves what knowledge, values, and experiences should be packed for the interplanetary, intergalactic trip that Parliament-Funkadelic told black people (and other audiences, too) to prepare for with their "mothership" metaphor. The next step in this synchronizing is to link texts and technologies so that the tradition, the present and the future, fit together—so that even if the intergalactic trip takes place at warp speed, black people will not continue to experience the same kinds of disruption and dislocation that have continually marked their experience in this land and have seemed to define transition from the victories of the civil rights and Black Power movements into the decades that followed.

No matter how badly many "back in the day" narratives beat up on Hip Hop, young people, and youth culture, Hip Hop offers us an important next step in that synchronizing or synthesizing. The very cultural expression that is so despised has been in a constant search for its roots, consciously and conspicuously linking past, present, and future through the sample and the mix. In other words, the key to addressing these tensions and the model creating the kinds of unities that can link print, oral, and digital texts, that can reconnect African Americans on both sides of the generational chasm in the search for fulfilling futures, is the DJ, the digital griot. By sampling funk and soul rhythms, melodies, harmonies, and lyrics, in its incessant layering, in its disruption of the linear narrative, Hip Hop—especially through the work of the DJ—helps heal the disruptions of black experience. The digital griot, in that same kind of constant searching that Nelson ascribes to Papa LaBas, remixes history to ensure that the soul and funk, Stax and Motown, getting paid and seeking change, civil rights and Black Power, Malcolm and Martin, stay alive and part of African American collective consciousness in ways that don't condemn us to either/or approaches. And ultimately, this is exactly the same challenge that the "back in the day" narrative is attempting to broker. The themes of the "back in the day" narrative show black people working diligently to resolve the tensions and debates that have always been central to African American rhetoric: participation or resistance, integration or nationalism. By locating the basis for an African American mythos for right now in the old school of the 1960s and 1970s, what is being created is a new groove, a new set of arguments about how to move forward that temporarily heals the dislocation, temporarily resolves the dialectic, offers a temporary synthesis for moving forward. The "back in the day" narrative becomes remix, sampling, layering, and revising multiple, sometimes contrasting elements of black culture in a productive synthesis for right now. Papa LaBas lives, and the range and diversity of African American experience live, even as people search for unities that can foster collective action.

The project of synchronizing African American rhetoric as an area of study to address the debates, tensions, differences, and commonalities across generations is one of connecting the crucial work of figures like Smitherman, Jacqueline Jones Royster, Keith Gilyard, Vivian Davis, Bill Cook, and many others with major questions related to technologies and writing and also technologies, community building, and communal goals. The careful work they have done in analyzing oral traditions, language, and discursive practices and in tying these traditions to questions of print literacies that have helped open up composition to a broader vision must be synched to the digital. Like the DJ lining up the beats and adjusting the equalizer before hitting the cross-fader, we must begin to line up the theoretical, ethical, and linguistic grooves to the questions of a changing same era to ensure smooth blends in the remix that is to come. We have to ask, What will it look like to apply Gilyard's and Victor Villanueva's innovations in the methodology of the autocritography to the experiences of growing up digital? Who will examine the uses of "wreck" as Gwen Pough describes it in YouTube battles around issues of race and representation? Who will find, describe, and analyze the online lyceums in ways that continue the trajectories that Royster and Shirley Wilson Logan have developed?

There are scholars cuing up the tracks: scholars like Vorris Nunley, Aesha Adams, Kermit Campbell, David Holmes, and Vershawn Young have begun spinning the arguments that continue the groove. Carmen Kynard, Annette Harris Powell, and Elaine Richardson have taken the groove and begun the remix in powerful ways. And the beats and harmonies that will create the next movement are falling into place from many different disciplinary spaces. One significant space for the looping, linking, and remixing of traditions and digital futures in academic work is eBlack, a movement emerging in black studies. In 2008, I was invited to participate in a group of fifteen information science professionals and scholars from across several disciplines to reimagine academic work and to develop a vision for black studies (both within the discipline and for scholars in other disciplinary homes). The initial impetus for the gathering, and much of the theoretical and practical foundation for our explorations, came from Abdul Alkalimat and Ron Bailey. While Alkalimat and Bailey provided much of the intellectual leadership in arranging the workshops, they fostered an egalitarian, collaborative approach to charting an agenda for eBlack studies, so that everyone participating contributed fully to the agenda without having to worry about whether their intellectual, activist, community, or professional interests might be filtered through long-standing orthodoxies. The resulting document, "eBlack: The Next Movement in Black Studies," goes a long way toward articulating the kind of remix I believe scholars in African American rhetoric, regardless of their disciplinary homes, should begin to pursue—not instead of but along with the powerful research agendas, questions, and lines of inquiry that currently mark study in the field:

> The term "eBlack Studies" describes the ongoing application of current digital information technology towards the production, dissemination, and collection of historical knowledge critical to the discipline of Black Studies and to the overall black experience. Thus, eBlack Studies, as it is now understood, is widely recognized to be at the forefront of research in Black Studies. Keeping this in mind, we—a group of Black Studies scholars from across the United States—first gathered together at the University of Illinois, Urbana-Champaign in July 2008 for the inaugural eBlack Studies workshop.
>
> The objectives of this workshop were twofold: to promote digital scholarship in Black Studies by building a cooperative research network, and to create an agenda for eBlack Studies within the academy as well as within the diverse communities where scholars of color presently work.
>
> The breadth and depth of work represented by the scholars gathered at this meeting broadly define the intersections of Black Studies and emerging issues of digital technology. Our intellectual, community, and activist interests include:

Afrofuturism, architecture, archival science and preservation, the Black Arts Movement, bibliometrics, critical race theory, cultural geography, cyberorganizing, ecotourism, environmental justice, genealogy, information seeking behaviors, information management, interpersonal communication, library and information science, public history and memory, rhetoric and composition, urban and regional planning, and US/Africa foreign policy. We have also committed ourselves to work in a number of related fields of study including but not limited to: Afro-Latin America and Latino/a Studies, Archaeology, Black Atlantic Studies, Black Queer Studies, Comparative Literature, Cultural Studies, Ethnomusicology, Psychology, Public Health, and Women's and Gender Studies.

As we chart the future of scholarship, teaching, and community work through the use of eBlack Studies, we acknowledge and celebrate our roots in the history and traditions of Black Studies, while at the same time, we enthusiastically embrace digital culture as it critically interrogates, interprets, defines, and documents the experiences of people of African descent. Furthermore, like Black Studies, eBlack Studies is unquestionably grounded in the everyday experiences of living Black communities, and is wholly committed to the preservation and accessibility of Black knowledge, history, experience, and perspective for the continued education of Black people and all people. We work to promote eBlack Studies as an interdisciplinary field of study of Black life and information communications technology across the African Diaspora based on an engaged model of praxis-centered, community advocacy. eBlack Studies will commit itself to knowledge creation and dissemination, dialogue, debate, engagement, and action in the interests of freedom for Black people in the US and the entire African Diaspora. As such, eBlack Studies will make a powerful contribution toward creating a better world for all peoples. eBlack Studies will work to cross the vast digital divide across ethnicities and transform the technological systems that structure Black life, as well as the patterns of political, economic, and power relations that influence technology design, production, and use.

We believe that eBlack Studies is a movement which is integral to the future of the discipline of Black Studies, and that this future will include utilizing, innovating, interrogating, critiquing, and where needed, resisting digital tools and spaces. As we chart this future, we believe that Library and Information Sciences are also essential to the development of eBlack Studies. Not only will eBlack Studies be the vanguard for work in Black Studies, it will also contribute to its future through the development of digital archives, while documenting the history of Black Studies and the Black experience.

We believe that eBlack Studies and Black Studies in general must reaffirm scholarly commitment to the wide-ranging diversity in Black experiences. As eBlack Studies holds promise to innovate and develop new directions for Black Studies, it also presents an opportunity to standardize our disciplinary procedures and policies as well as to rejuvenate our pedagogy and practice. The innovations we collectively achieve in these areas will offer unique possibilities for other disciplines as well. Finally, the weaving of Black Studies and new information technologies offers profound possibilities for the future of the field, including:

- Preservation of the many modes and facets of the Black experience in digitally archived, easily accessible, open source formats
- Collaborative, interdisciplinary approaches to scholarship, teaching, and learning
- Intersectional approaches to scholarship and action, emphasizing the linkages that persist among class, sexuality, nationality and forms of oppression, while promoting strategies for action and liberation
- The aggregation and compilation of reports from the outposts of struggle throughout the world providing testimony to scholars, activists, and laypeople

- The active pursuit of connections with scholars of the Black experience and practitioners in areas such as the hard sciences, computer sciences, history of science, engineering, media studies, economics, media production, performance studies, fine arts, and other disciplines not typically associated with work in Black Studies. New ways of imagining connection and kinship must also engage with professional organizations such as the National Society of Black Engineers (NSBE), National Association of Black Journalists (NABJ), transnational grassroots organizations, and non governmental organizations. We must work to insure that an understanding of the Black experience be more than a mere conversation among academics.
- Utilization of all the available means of digital technologies such as social networking, data mining, the Internet, and others engaged in our scholarship, teaching, curriculum development, and community engagement, not just for our own personal and professional purposes, but to strengthen connections with Black communities throughout the world.

Interrogation and critique of technological systems and tools.

- Advocacy as well as description in our intellectual work.
- Utilization of models of scholarship and engagement that reach beyond traditional academic work and academic systems of financing, reward, and recognition.

We are witnessing an information revolution—a revolution that is leading global transformation. People of African descent have always played pivotal roles in the history of technological revolutions—sometimes as innovators and inventors, more frequently as laborers—and their labor permitted the wealth that spurred further technological advances. The social consequences of today's information revolution include the suffering and economic insecurity of African Americans and others in the African diaspora and also dislocations among others in society. Our communities have been digitally divided, but we are dedicating ourselves to serve as a bridge over the river of that divide. Our social values are cyberdemocracy, collective intelligence, and information freedom. We embrace the information revolution and dedicate our scholarship to academic excellence and social responsibility. We welcome others to join us in this endeavor.

Of course, the manifesto as a genre has its difficulties as well as its strengths, and the work that emerges from a group in an originary moment will always, must always, evolve from that original declaration, as examinations of movements like the Harlem Renaissance, the Combahee River Collective, and the Black Arts Movement attest. My concern here is with the collective vision that shaped this document and with a framing of eBlack studies as a remix of traditional narratives that synchronizes innovation and tradition, marking a new moment and a new set of questions by announcing its firm commitment to do so in solidarity with, in relationship to, that which has come before. The sharp differences in the substance, rhetorical stance, and delivery between a statement like this and the Sharpton/Glaude debate and the "back in the day" narrative could not be more stark, though this narrative form, Sharpton, and Glaude all create the kind of dialectical tension that allows syntheses like these to emerge.

"Every generation must, out of relative obscurity, find its mission, fulfill it, or betray it." There will always be tensions between generations, and those tensions are pronounced among African Americans between the so-called civil rights and Hip Hop generations. At some point, Eddie Glaude will be the resident oldhead on the scene telling another generation of young lions that they've got it wrong. And while the "back in the day" narrative reflects frustration and negative assumptions on both sides of the generational chasm, the fact that many generations, from youth to elders, have embraced it also reflects the Afrofuturistic potential of Papa LaBas, reflects the transformative synthesis that Hip Hop gave American culture with the sample and the remix, and shows an active hunger from both elders and youngfolk, to rememory, reclaim, and reconnect. This potential can lead to the kind of exchange that can link the old, old story with new technologies, can bring souls aged in struggle together with young lions and their new fire and new visions in that continual search for higher ground.

Shoutout: Cyber-Church (www.cyber-church.us)

This digital griot project, housed by eBlack studies at the University of Illinois at Urbana-Champaign and created and maintained by Abdul Alkalimat, uses the historical ties between African Americans and the institution of the black church in the attempt to improve technology access and to counter the legacies of oppression. The home page for the site announces these goals immediately: "We are a bridge over the digital divide. We are beginning our journey among God's children suffering the legacy of slavery. Our journey is to embrace everyone." The site seeks to be a repository for church information and materials for people from all faiths anywhere in the world but with a particular focus on African Americans. One of Alkalimat's goals in creating the site and fostering the community that is growing within it is to develop a research tool that enables scholars to work with searchable data sets of thousands and thousands of texts, from which larger patterns and connections about black life can be gleaned, as opposed to having the study of the textures and contours of black life and experience limited to readings of small numbers of texts because of problems of availability. The site includes information on major theologians and organizations like seminaries, publication houses, and denominations. In addition, one can search for church programs, sermons, archives, newsletters, and other materials by church locations, names, or search terms or strings within the documents.

4

Mixtape: Black Theology's Mixtape Movement at Forty

> So far the Black church has remained conspicuously silent, continuing its business as usual. The holding of conferences, the election of bishops, the fund-raising drive for a new building or air conditioner seem to be more important than the Blacks who are shot because they want to be human. The Black church, though spatially located in the community, has not responded to the needs of the people. It has, rather, drained the community, seeking to be more and more like the white church. Its ministers have condemned the hopeless and have mimicked the values of whites. For this reason most Black power people bypass the church as irrelevant to their objectives.
>
> —James Cone, Black Theology and Black Power

> Following my presentation on "Black women's literature as Sacred Texts," Dr. Johnson Reagon commented that I live out the essence of my name by always opening up the canon. I attempted to dodge the responsibility of this authoritative task by explaining that I am a "cannon" boom! boom! Dr. Johnson Reagon remarked, "We are an oral people. A cannon is a canon." Indeed.
>
> —Katie Cannon, Katie's Canon: Womanism and the Soul of the Black Community

"WHO YOU WIT!?!?!?" was one of late comedian Bernie Mac's favorite opening lines and refrains. Far more than merely a bold, brash line to announce his presence on the stage, Mac entered the messiness of our current, allegedly post-everything moment and immediately called *the* question for his primarily (though by no means completely) black audiences. In three words, he demanded that audiences locate and identify themselves and declare their allegiances and simultaneously presented his own positionality. Bradford T. Stull's important book *Amid the Fall, Dreaming of Eden: Du Bois, King, Malcolm X, and Emancipatory Composition* begins with a version of the same question posed with a directness and urgency similar to Mac's: "Stated bluntly, immediately, with no appeal to narrative descriptions of oppression, of emancipation, of pain, of joy, here is the question that drives this book: What is the sociopolitical telos of composition studies? Or, put more simply, whom, what, does composition serve?" (1).

In asking those of us in the field to begin any inquiry having similarly located ourselves and our ethical commitments, Stull argues that current discourse in the field allows for what amounts to three choices: to teach students to uphold the status quo of American ideologies in writing instruction, to declare neutrality in the debates over the political and ethical issues involved in language and writing, or to base one's work in a commitment to changing the current system, to align oneself "with the belief that the study of composition can, should, help set the captives free and give sight to the blind" (2). In articulating his idea of what an emancipatory composition might mean and look like, Stull grounds his vision in the compositional educations, practices, and texts of W. E. B. Du Bois, Martin Luther King Jr., and Malcolm X. Stull, arguing that each of these figures represents this approach to composition because their composing practices are at the same time conservative and extreme, adopts a Burkean "comic attitude" in taking the tropes, commonplaces, and language practices central to American democracy and using them toward the ends of liberation. Of course, Stull's invocation of Kenneth Burke here also evokes Cornel West's call for a sense of the tragicomic and thus Ralph Ellison's classic definition of the blues: "The blues is an impulse to keep the painful details and episodes of a brutal experience alive in one's aching consciousness, to finger its jagged edge, and transcend it—not by the mere contemplation of philosophy, but by wringing from it a near tragic, near comic lyricism" (78).

The comic attitude that allows Du Bois, King, and X to confront the tragedies in a brutal experience and, through a sense of irony, to flip the discursive practices of a language system implicated in those tragedies is "radically theopolitical" according to Stull, because their approach to composition simultaneously "roots itself in the foundational theological and political language of the American experience. It is radically theopolitical, on the other hand, because as it does so, it calls into question this language and thus the American experience itself. Hence, it is at once conservative and extreme" (3). Stull is interested, therefore, in the synthesis of access and transformation, in knowing the codes and in flipping them in the interests of people those codes were never intended to serve, in the synchronization of tradition and innovation.

My first conscious thoughts about a mixtape of any kind were in the summer of 1983, recording songs off of *Club Style*, a Hip Hop radio program that came on Saturday nights on WDMT, 107.9, a local radio station in Cleveland. In my own "back in the day" narratives that my friends and I share about growing up in Cleveland in the 1970s and 1980s, we reminisce about football games or dozens sessions that stopped promptly at 6:55 on Saturday nights, no matter what the score, no matter how heated the competition, so we could all run in the house to listen to and record Johnny O's twenty-minute workout, an extended set of one of Cleveland's real DJ Heroes cutting, scratching, mixing, and remixing songs and breaks. Initially we just wanted to record those workout sessions, marveling at Johnny O's skills on the wheels, enamored with what was clearly a whole new game musically. But this simple move of straight bootlegging (which, I should note, led to props in the everyday knowledge economy of preteen and adolescent kids in the neighborhood and at school, because O played songs that weren't in rotation anywhere else on the radio) quickly morphed into an art of creation through selection, arrangement, and compilation: we would record and arrange the songs *we* liked the most from *Club Style* or Jeffrey Charles's *For Lovers Only* slow jam session every night, or anywhere else on the radio. The challenges of having to wait for the songs we liked and attempting to capture the entire song before the DJ cut to another song or commercial or began to talk over the outro were nothing compared to the fun of feeling like we had become DJs, able to select our favorite songs and arrange and compile them in some way that was ours, that reflected our own growing tastes and personalities.

So in the hands of everyday people, the mixtape was an act of vernacular canon formation, deeply personal yet also a part of public conversation, as other young people talked about their favorite songs, new releases they thought others didn't know yet, their staunchly defended positions about who were the best artists, singers, and MCs, and their own idiosyncratic ways of choosing and arranging the tracks. Even in our junior high school hands, these anthologies became about the challenge of imposing order on the chaos—the challenge of getting everything that mattered on the two sides of those sixty- or ninety-minute cassettes. But while millions of young people of all races engaged in these everyday acts of collage and canon formation creating party tapes, "slow grind" tapes, road trip tapes, "greatest of alllll time" tapes, and who knows how many other varieties, DJs in the Hip Hop game turned the genre into their own art form that circulated in underground and gift economies and challenged the taste-making authority of payola-corrupted corporate media and copyright law that always seemed to side with big money.

Jeff "Chairman" Mao helps to document the phenomenon of the mixtape, its importance to Hip Hop, and the ways it reflects the difficulty that lies in the tensions between access, resistance, and aims for transformation in an article anthologized in the *Vibe History of Hip Hop*. Mao leads up to his interview with legendary DJ and community-builder Afrika Bambaataa by describing one of Bam's classic mixtapes, *Death Mix Live!!*, recorded at the Bronx's Monroe High School in 1983 and released in 1987:

> Within the recording's less than 20 minute running time, New York's famed "Master of records," along with right-hand spin-ster DJ Jazzy Jay, charts a typically adventurous, unabashedly sloppy course through the land of Hip Hop break-beats; an exploration that epitomizes the renegade spirit of the music's pioneering programmers. The Motown effervescence of the

Jackson 5's "It's Great to Be Here" bumps beats with the synthetic, Japanese new wave dance rhythms of the Yellow Magic Orchestra's "Computer Game," the cowbell stomp of soul journeyman Vernon Burch's "Get Up" . . . and even collides into Grandmaster Flash and the Furious Five's kinetic debut single "Superrappin." All the while, the Echo-plexing voices of unidentified MCs declare props-over-here Zulu superiority on Bam's behalf for anyone within hearing distance. (70)

One of the points that Mao's description of Bambaataa's classic mixtape makes is that even while DJs use and arrange other sources in the compilation, they are much more than compilers: they are artists expected to innovate through their own artistic vision that leads to the elements chosen, how they're mixed and layered, and how they build and speak to various conversations and communities inside the DJ and Hip Hop game. Mao compares the technological, sonic, and cultural innovation of the "Bronx mixing OG's [original gangsters] and their effect on future generations" to artists like Jimi Hendrix, Muddy Waters, and Chuck Berry (71). Just as a literary or a scholarly anthology is supposed to make some kind of statement in its scholarly conversation, the mixtape must as well.

In addition to building the primary track of my own intellectual mixtape on the explicit linking of Malcolm X and Martin Luther King Jr., of access and transformation that Stull advocates, this chapter seeks to build on Stull's argument and extend it, through an exploration of the rhetorical practices of the one movement in African American freedom struggle that was explicitly created as an attempt to synthesize the ideological continuum between integration (or radical democracy) and black nationalisms. Black Theology, the movement built on the legacy and synthesis of King and X, represents a mixtape movement because it links or loops together many of the tracks or narratives that mark African American history and the rhetorical tradition that emerges from it. Malcolm and Martin, radical democracy and black nationalism, a vision of the Beloved Community for the nation and world and of healthy black communities able to love each other and embrace blackness and black history—Black Theology's other tracks respond to many of the other continua in the tradition that are often mistaken as either/or binaries:

- old school/new school—tradition and innovation
- Saturday night and Sunday morning—street and church, secular and sacred
- the black community and the Beloved Community
- the block and the rock—a commitment to addressing local, national, and transnational issues
- specificities in black experiences and issues and searing intersectional interrogation and critique of sexism, racism, and class and sex oppression
- radical democracy and black nationalisms
- public discourse and vernacular traditions/practices in the underground
- disciplinary and interdisciplinary concerns

In lining up the beats, lines, melodies, harmonies, tracks, and traditions that I'm arguing can lead to a new conception of both composition and African American rhetoric in a new era (a digital era that leads us to believe that we are *always* in a new era), the loopings and layerings I advocate seem arbitrary or undisciplined, an attempt to throw everything into the gumbo, or the mixtape, to maintain this chapter's metaphor and frame. To some extent, this is an intentional stylistic move, an argument for eclecticism, for range as well as depth, in scholarly work. But just as the mixtape imposes order on the chaos through the particular cuts and blends and arrangements it uses, understanding Black Theology as a mixtape movement can help to allay these concerns because its intentional synthesizing of important tensions as a guiding principle and postures of careful reflexivity and self-critique do not result in a stasis-eroding, strong postmodern relativism that—for me, at least—erodes rhetorical agency. After all, no matter how complex the questions or ranging positions or issues, one must ever, always, take a stand. Courses must be designed, assignments created, curricula established, budget and personnel priorities set, even in the most narrow views of the field or academic work one might hold. Black Theology, studied as a movement, is a powerful example of an intellectual and activist mixtape because its commitment to working across the whole range of continua that mark black experience and struggle does not hinder an ethical clarity that allows it to always answer Bernie Mac's (and Bradford Stull's) question "Who you wit!?!?!?" and thus allow for individual and collective action. Consistent as the downbeat, or The One, that brings these tracks together, that makes such wide-ranging syntheses and synchronizations possible, is an unwavering commitment to stand in solidarity with the oppressed and to develop theoretical and activist agendas that serve the broader society even while working to transform it to foster freedom and equality for those who have been denied them.

As with the mix and the remix, others have already begun to consider the rhetorical possibilities for the mixtape in digital writing, and in composition generally. Geoffrey Sirc's keynote lecture at the 2007 Computers and Writing Conference at Wayne State University is often regarded as one of the most compelling treatments of the form's potential role for compositionists to date. In the talk, Sirc argued for compositionists to have a greater appreciation for the role of selection, combination, and arrangement in writing and to let go of an unnecessary, overdetermined emphasis on content in writing instruction. Alex Reid, one of the scholars I saw at the conference, blogged about Sirc's lecture, capturing his impression of it this way: "Sirc discusses the selection process [at work in creating a mixtape] in terms of the sublime, flow, and a sense of the cool. That is, how do you know to make a good mixtape? Put simply, you just have to put together songs that sound cool. Then I suppose there are other rhetorical considerations depending on the occasion of the mixtape" ("Geoffrey Sirc").

Yes, I suppose there are some other rhetorical considerations at work, too. Many more. I think Reid's characterization of Sirc's argument is right on—Sirc advocates a sense of play, and writers have the ability to choose whatever combinations they want in the pursuit of an affective "cool." In this respect, Sirc's argument is very similar to that which Jeff Rice makes advocating for the sample as a valuable concept for composition pedagogy. And while I see value in both Rice's and Sirc's arguments in favor of the ability to play freely in texts and techniques in the writing classroom, their desire to lift, sample, and loop concepts from black traditions freely for their mere applicability without concern for the culture or context that produced them, the mixtape as rhetorical practice offers composition pedagogy and digital writing theory far more than a whimsical pursuit of the cool. Even the notion of the cool, however, has cultural and political roots in black culture and rhetoric that we would be wise to trace and explore. From the facility, ease, and seemingly unaffected postures in slave-era practices like shuckin' and jiving, through the blues and Miles Davis's classic intervention into jazz with *The Birth of the Cool*, and into Hip Hop, "cool" in African American culture reflects an aesthetic, an epistemology, and a set of survival practices grounded in black folklore and narrative traditions. Fred Brathwaite, aka Fab Five Freddy of *Wild Style* and *Yo! MTV Raps* fame, explains the importance of cool in Hip Hop culture. In an introductory essay to Jamel Shabazz's photographic tribute to Hip Hop, *Back in the Days*, Fab notes that cool isn't just some vague affect that helps people feel good, but rather it's

> all about having the right flavor and savoir faire. Such a style blended a certain kind of rebelliousness with a casual nonchalance. It was a cocky confidence of sorts that was meticulously updated by a perpetual pursuit of an alternative, yet distinct sensibility. Cool permeated the scene. Kool Herc, LL Cool J, Cool Rock Ski, and Kool Moe Dee were but a few of the countless numbers who added the word cool to their street, graffiti, DJ, MC, and break dancer names. But cool back then went beyond the Kangols, Adidas, gold chains, monikers, and the sheer superficiality of our current "bling bling" counterculture. It went much deeper. . . . Cool was—and in many cases still is—about survival. Like the images Jamel shows us, cool was about strength, pride, courage, and a fierce love of self. (6)

By citing Robert Farris Thompson's analysis of cool in Benin and Yoruba cultures in his classic *Flash of the Spirit* and bringing it full circle to Huey Newton and Stokely Carmichael, Fab presents the cool of Hip Hop and the DJ that Sirc, Rice, Stuart Selber, and Johndan Johnson-Eilola tap into as linking Africa and the diaspora, tradition and innovation, and at least the possibility of survival, dignity, and resistance. Now, how Rice is able to claim that he "invented" a rhetoric of something, much less a rhetoric of the cool (*Rhetoric of Cool* 5, 113), given Fab's description and many of the texts he himself cites, I have no idea, though the various traditions he links together in his study of cool help make the book an intriguing one. My playful rib of Rice aside, though, I believe that the mixtape—when connected to a conversation about the ethical dimensions of the practice and the folk culture that led us there through the oral tradition and the DJ's griotic, technological preservation of and intervention in that tradition—offers us a framework for navigating the difficult binaries and tensions inherent in the task of writing in digital spaces and offers at least the possibility for the kind of emancipatory composition Stull argues for.

It would be foolish to romanticize any of the rhetorical practices that fall under the wide cover of the digital griot: the sample, the mix, the remix, the mixtape, and the bootleg are all fraught with difficult ethical questions tugging at the central tensions in African American rhetoric. Copyright or copyleft, participation or resistance, integration or nationalism, civil rights or Black Power. The genres and practices of the DJ have always been caught up in the same systems of power and capital as any other element in African American rhetoric, to such an extent that the mixtape and the DJ as a figure have been subject to their own "back in the day" narratives. One such reflection calls significant attention to the ethical questions always present in any rhetorical performance. Afrika Bambaataa and Grandmaster DXT (also known as D.ST, the DJ who pushed Grandmaster Flash's and Grand Wizard Theodore's innovations with the scratch into new territory and raised an entire nation's consciousness of the DJ as a musician in his 1983 collaboration with Herbie Hancock on the Grammy-winning "Rockit") draw a sharp if double-edged distinction between a moment when Hip

Hop and the DJ's craft were more committed to and reflective of an African American cultural underground. "Making rap records tore everything apart. . . . It tore all of us apart. That's what killed Hip Hop. . . . As far as the culture, it was over. 'Cause money took over and the people who had no knowledge of the culture but had better knowledge of the business aspect got control of the shit and messed it up" (Mao with Bambaataa 74). Bambaataa cosigns DXT's frustration in his interview with Mao but notes the complicated relationships involved in the DJ's move to the mainstream. Some DJs sold out, allowing their art to become an instrument of global capitalism, authenticating industry artists for fans expecting artists to have developed "street credibility." Others wanted to see Hip Hop grow to influence national and international audiences, sharing their work willingly with any and all available audiences. And yet others were lured into mainstream spaces after the corporate presence had already become a major force in the Hip Hop game. "I had a vision," Bambaataa told Mao. "A lot of other people were selfish and wanted to hold stuff to theyselves. I had a vision to try to make this a whole world phenomenon and movement . . . and everything fell in place" (74). Mao traces the rest of the history of the mixtape as art form in the hands of Hip Hop DJs, noting that it played many different roles: call and response debates over aesthetics; an exhibition of an individual DJ's technical skills and knowledge of music; a flashpoint in debates over intellectual property as recording industry executives simultaneously wanted to shut down the practice through legal action and yet enlist DJs to create mixtapes to create buzz and provide vernacular authenticity for their chosen artists (translation: yet another version of payola); and demonstrations of rhetorical ability as DJs used them to show just how hard they could rock a party, using either live sets or mixtapes meant to simulate a live set. After discussing masters of the art form like Kid Capri, Jam Master Jay, DJ Premier, Biz Markie, Luvbug Starski, the Beat Junkies, and the Invisibl Skratch Piklz (and providing a great discography of classic mixtapes), Mao sums up the tensions this way: "Hip Hop's Darwinian cycle of natural selection has placed its ruthless mack hand down on virtually every discipline of the culture in some way, yet it is DJ-ing which has somehow managed to transcend, reinvent, survive, and flourish" (77).

Of course, these very difficulties and dualities mark the current moment for composition as a discipline in the academy and the public arena as well as in African American rhetoric. We often struggle with the tensions between wanting our work to have real-world relevance for the audiences and communities we care about, attracted to bell hooks's or Cornel West's or Angela Davis's model of the public intellectual and working to earn greater respect throughout academic spaces that cling to claims that our work is little more than a necessary service—and therefore evil—to the rest of the university. The questions that Afrika Bambaataa raises about the ethics that guide or should guide the DJ's work are being asked in all spaces of African American culture as well, and it is this search for greater unity and greater commitment to collective work and activism that is a crucial factor in the "back in the day" narrative. More than forty years after the chief victories of the civil rights movement and the nationalist challenge posed by organizations like the Student Non-violent Coordinating Committee, the Black Panthers, and the nation of Islam, the African American community remains standing as voices crying in the wilderness—and the broader nation remains a wilderness crying for a voice. From Chris Rock's joke that after the deaths of Malcolm X and Martin Luther King, "we need a leader. All we got now is a bunch of substitute teachers!" to Cornel West's plea in the 2006 State of Black America, "What are we going to do about this suffering?," African Americans across poor, working, middle and even upper-middle classes have wondered where the voices are in our communities that are fearless, powerful, and focused on liberation for black people. This longing comes across not only in the "back in the day" narrative but also in street-level and academic critiques of Hip Hop and other elements of popular culture, in assessments of education, community life, and the church. This longing for liberating voices, actions, and movements was especially pronounced in the aftermath of Hurricanes Katrina and Rita, when African Americans all over the country criticized not only local, state, and national governments but also

African American organizations and leaders for not doing more to organize masses of black people to serve and work to minimize the suffering of people in Louisiana and Mississippi.

While people across all segments of black communities express this longing, however, African American popular and political culture seems to have been trapped in a space that demands that people merely cut the best deal they can within a corrupt social, economic, and political structure. Thus, the questions that Afrika Bambaataa raises about the ethics that guide or should guide the DJ's work evoke long-standing debates within African American rhetoric. Further, the textual layering and the narrative and generational synthesis that are central to the rhetorical forms of the DJ's craft call into question the theme of synthesis itself. In a moment where the tensions between participation and resistance are so fraught with difficulty, and in a tradition that is often read through the lens of steep ideological divides, are there moments or movements that genuinely bring together participation, resistance, and the larger goal of transformation? While many historians have debunked the idea that any movement or activist can be read as a pure exemplar of any one ideology, the debates between integrationist, nationalist, and class-based transformation have been pitched, from at least as early as the convention movement of the nineteenth century to the present. Black Theology is one movement that takes us beyond the polemic, that offers a model of synthesis that is not simply a matter of Hegelian agonistic postures leading to a new idea but a blending and layering of the many ideological tracks of black freedom struggle into a coherent, committed whole—a mixtape movement that offers a new lens for examining some of the ethical issues at the center of writing and writing instruction in a digital, multimedia age.

Black Theology, a movement whose roots run throughout African American history and across to Africa but started as an explicit movement with the 1966 National Committee of Negro Clergymen's (later renamed the National Conference of Black Clergy) "Black Power Statement" and the 1969 publication of James Cone's *Black Theology and Black Power*, began with the explicit intention of bridging generational, class, and ideological divides among black people. By labeling it a "mixtape movement," I argue that Black Theology is the one movement in the tradition of black freedom struggle whose cause was clearly defined by the desire to literally synthesize, layer, and blend Malcolm and Martin, radical democratic and nationalist impulses, a focus on domestic and black diasporic concerns. The remainder of this chapter will examine the ways Black Theology as theorized by James Cone and Katie Cannon achieves this rhetoric of synthesis and articulates an ethics that can address the many layered challenges of African American rhetoric, and writing instruction, in a digital age—and can support a truly transformative access to technology.

By arguing that Black Theology can offer us a different lens through which to view digital ethics issues, I mean that the movement offers a set of principles that can guide thinking, teaching, and doing with and about writing and technology and can enable African Americans to use technologies on their own terms and in their own individual and collective interests. It can also allow writing teachers, students, and scholars space for both participation in and resistance to the many constraints imposed on us by copyright laws and intellectual property conventions. Carefully considered, it might even lead us to a bootleg, copyleft, open source composition. The search for such principles is fraught with difficulty in a moment that seems to demand assimilation as the price of access, but Black Theology's history and current practice offer the possibility of both access and transformation. Grounding a discussion of digital ethics for African Americans in the theoretical frame of Black Theology as a mixtape movement, or a rhetoric of synthesis allowing both access and transformation, would encourage black people to make use of technological systems and tools toward the following goals: an insistence on racial justice; a deep abiding love for black people in the United States, on the African continent, and throughout the diaspora; a commitment to stand in solidarity with other groups of people who are and have been systematically oppressed; a searing critique of sexism, class-based exploitation, and homophobia; and an intellectual honesty that demands self-critique as well as systemic critique and an unflinching willingness to confront the major, difficult questions—and the changes—that every era presents without taking refuge in nostalgia.

I should be clear about my intentions in taking up the preacher as griot and Black Theology as a theoretical source for African American rhetoric and technology access. I do not pretend to study the movement or the sermon as either a theologian or a homiletician. My interest in the possibilities of liberation theology for current struggle and how themes of liberation are alive and present in the black sermon is a rhetorical interest, asking the same questions that I would ask of the blues, Hip Hop, political speeches, black women's essayistic practices, or any other genre or site of rhetorical study: How have black people used language to get free? How have they defined freedom? How does one make the argument, raise consciousness, develop unity, and move people to action?

To put the issue differently, much scholarly attention has been given to the study of the performative elements of the black sermon and the discursive forms that make it such a special element of the African American vernacular tradition. My interest, instead, is in how this movement and this genre deal with the difficult questions of liberation. How does one get people willing to act for the sake of freedom? How does one move people beyond their fears, beyond their sense that the systemic nature of racism makes the problems too big, beyond the resignation that leads people to take comfort in status and material things? Once one has created an imperative for action, how does he or she bridge sharp ideological differences to develop unities capable of taking action? Finally, with respect to Black Theology as a movement, how has it developed in the midst of all of the influences that would silence the prophetic voice of the black preacher, so that there are still those who believe and preach liberation right here and now rather than raise money for buildings that might or might not get built or extol some pie-in-the-sky religion that asks people to suffer patiently now but still pay for the preacher's Cadillac?

Because of the centrality of the African American church in freedom struggle—and, at times, in conservative tolerance of and even participation in the oppression of African Americans—even a secular scholar cannot ignore the importance of the church as a site of rhetorical study and the sermon as a crucial genre in charting the rhetorical history of African Americans. Just as the mixtape reflects the complex relationship between resistance and participation, the African American sermon is yet another demonstration of that classic Du Boisian trope, double consciousness. It is at once the most revered and the most parodied genre in the black rhetorical tradition, with almost every literary or vernacular writer in that tradition either paying tribute to, being informed by, reacting against, overtly satirizing, or indirectly critiquing it, and sometimes all of the above. For a student of rhetoric, it is in some moments a wonderful example of agency, ethics, and engagement, and in some others, the epitome of charlatanism, self-importance, insubstantial performance, and the abuse of commonplaces in the promotion of self-interest. It operates completely within the African American cultural underground where outsiders often have little or no idea of the complex epistemological, theological, and linguistic codes that enable the preacher and congregation to come together to literally make word flesh and flesh word, and yet it is perhaps the genre that has given African Americans the greatest entrée into public discourse in the attempt to both gain access to and at the same time fundamentally transform America.

William Wiggins identifies the black preacher as *the* master griot in African American culture. In his essay "The Black Preacher as Storyteller," Wiggins uses the Tar Baby as metaphor to explain both the preacher's mastery of the griot's craft and the depth of black people's relationship to this figure. He says the preacher's "verbal artistry covers Afro-American communal life like the briar patch did Brer Rabbit" (209) and that the relationship between African Americans and the preacher is pivotal in the culture, in sacred and secular spaces alike. He notes it as "irrefutable . . . that the masses of Black people are stuck as tightly to their storytelling Black preachers as Brer Rabbit was to the Tar Baby" (210). This griot is far more than one who brings scripture to a congregation; he or she is the person who is trusted to tell and interpret cultural history through current events and to chart visions for the future. A proof of the importance of the preacher as griot and the sermon to this rhetorical tradition lies in its reach and influence outside the church, where people often invoke both the institution and the sermon, both playfully and seriously, in order to move people.

Black literary, vernacular, and popular cultural texts are so replete with odes to, struggles with, critiques of, and love for the African American sermon as to resoundingly shout to the student or critic that one cannot understand this culture or its discursive features or rhetorical production without deep and sustained study of this genre. From the loving, prodding parodies of the *Flip Wilson Show*'s "The Church of What's Happening Now" and Richard Pryor's characters in *Car Wash* and *Which Way Is Up?*, to James Weldon Johnson's poetic tribute *God's Trombones* (which is still taught, recited, and performed in many black communities) and Ossie Davis's warm and layered portrayal in *Purlie Victorious*, to what might be the most beautiful and compelling treatment I've read in any literary work in Baby Suggs's sermon in the clearing in Toni Morrison's *Beloved*, to literally thousands of other references, reflections, and reexaminations in songs, scholarship, and the streets, to the rich intertextuality and signifyin of thousands of sermons themselves, there is far too much comment on the black sermon to single out any number of treatments as most important. For the purposes of this chapter, however, my focus is on the rhetorical challenges of liberation for the preacher—how those preachers take the themes of Black Theology and bring them to the sermon and how the ethical commitments and rhetorical practices of these griots can encourage transformative work with technologies.

What is Black Theology? The short answer to this question is that Black Theology is one manifestation of a broader movement called liberation theology, that it is an understanding of the Christian faith that insists that God is on the side of the oppressed and that one's faith must be made manifest in a willingness to work for the freedom of people right here, right now, rather than believing in an otherworldly, "we'll understand it better by and by" notion of faith. Black Theology insists that Christ was first and foremost a liberator and that God takes sides in the events of human history. Black Theology also insists that any religious faith must be accountable to the history, needs, and future of the people it serves, and therefore, for black people, it must embrace and celebrate black history. Finally, for the short answer, Black Theology is a movement that has always been present in the black church in the voices of people like Harriet Tubman, James Varick, Harriet Jacobs, Henry McNeal Turner, Frederick Douglass, and David Walker and in many, many others who refused to accept the assumption that Christianity justified slavery, beginning as an organized, public movement on July 31, 1966, when a collection of black clergy began to bring together the ideas of both Martin Luther King Jr. and Malcolm X in order to forge a faith and an intellectual movement that were relevant to the contemporary contexts of both civil rights and Black Power.

James Cone, often acknowledged as the first to build and articulate a specifically black liberation theology with his 1969 and 1970 books *Black Theology and Black Power* and *A Black Theology of Liberation*, establishes this theological outlook on the combination of Martin Luther King's and Malcolm X's thinking and practice. Throughout his life and career, Cone has argued that Malcolm X is as important to theology and to black religious faith as King and demands that theology be built on the combination of intellectual work and activism in the world. Cone continues the argument in his 1984 book *For My People* that people cannot just lean on the esoteric ruminations of theologians interpreting Jesus' words but must identify with whom he calls the "Man Jesus," the life and work of Christ that made real his gospel through the liberation of the oppressed. In other words, the gospel is social, rooted in life right here, right now; the spiritual life is utterly about one's being in this world and not just thoughts about another world in heaven. Cone puts it this way:

> The kingdom of God which the poor may enter is not merely an eschatological longing for escape to a transcendent reality, nor is it an inward serenity that eases unbearable suffering.

Rather, it is God encountering man in the very depths of his being-in-the-world and releasing him from all human evils, like racism, which hold him captive. The repentant man knows that even though God's ultimate kingdom is in the future, it breaks through even now like a ray of light upon the darkness of the oppressed. (9)

Cone proceeds to make a point that would be dangerous for some, even downright heretical to others: "When we make it contemporaneous with our life situation, Jesus' message is clear enough. The message of Black Power is the message of Christ himself" (9).

One reason for Cone's insistence that Malcolm and Martin, civil rights and Black Power, be linked is his desire to repair a rupture in the African American rhetorical situation, to reclaim the right to speak boldly, clearly, prophetically in an environment that has never tolerated bold African American critique—the right to a righteous disgust with the intransigence of racism and systematic exclusions tied to race. Addressing the tendency of some religious figures and others in the society to label such anger or indignation "hate," as the entire Black Theology movement was labeled in 2008 based on a willful misinterpretation of sound bites from Reverend Jeremiah Wright played on an endless loop by many media outlets, Cone says in the introduction to *Black Theology and Black Power*: "Black Power is the most important development in American life in this century. . . . Even in its most radical expression, is not the antithesis of Christianity, nor is it a heretical idea to be tolerated with painful forbearance" (1). He presses his claim for the righteous indignation of one who loves his country dearly, even in its intransigence: "This work, then is written with a definite attitude, the attitude of an angry Black man, disgusted with the oppression of Black people in America and with the scholarly demand to be 'objective' about it. Too many people have died, and too many are on the edge of death" (2). Gwen Pough comes to mind yet again in Cone's insistence on the right to rebel and in his linking of Black Power with civil rights in developing Black Theology. In her book *Check It While I Wreck It: Black Womanhood, Hip-Hop Culture, and the Public Sphere*, Pough offers the concept of "wreck" to link the work of black women Hip Hop artists to figures throughout African American history. Black women often have to "bring wreck" to force an entrance into discourses that would limit or deny them. Over and over again, in the messages American society sends black people as a whole, or in the messages society and often black men send black women, the idea persists that one must choose to affirm the discursive rules and conventions of structures that deny one's humanity as the cost of participation in such discourse. Cone, like Pough after him, refuses to accept such silencing.

Black Theology demands that people choose sides in the events and forces that lead to systematic oppression. Whether it finds its biblical basis in the story of the Israelites being delivered from slavery or in Christ's ministry to the poor and outcasts of society, Black Theology is a redefinition of Christianity that challenges any concept of life that allows people to remain complicit in the oppression of others. One important element of this challenge is the rejection of neutrality. King preached and wrote incessantly that one cannot be against oppression but silent in the face of that oppression. The key here is that Black Theology as a movement does not talk about the poor or rationalize why they are poor but takes a word to the poor, to those who are oppressed, and proclaims freedom and the right of people to define their own realities even as they transform those realities. Cone puts the theme of transformation this way:

> It means the irruption of a new age, an age that has to do with God's action in history on behalf of man's salvation. It is an age of liberation, in which "the blind receive their sight, the lame walk, the lepers are cleansed, the deaf hear, the dead are raised up, the poor have the good news preached to them." This is not pious talk, and one does not need a seminary degree to interpret the passage. It is a message about the ghetto, Vietnam, and all other injustices done in the name of democracy and religion to further the social, political, and economic affairs of the oppressor. In Christ, God enters human affairs and takes sides with the oppressed. Their suffering becomes

his suffering, their despair, divine despair. Through Christ, the poor are offered freedom now to rebel against that which makes them other than human. (*Black Theology* 8)

There are four important messages here: God is on the side of the oppressed; one must choose sides; Christianity is about more than individual salvation—that salvation means the liberation of black people; and suffering people have a right to rebel against those forces that oppress them. Cone is also clear that Black Theology is not merely an indictment of the racism and conservatism of the white religious establishment. He also issues withering critique of the black church, arguing that it is incompetent and irrelevant for many black people: "How else can we explain that some church fellowships are more concerned with nonsmoking principles or temperances than with children who die of rat bites or men who are shot while looting a television set? Men are dying of hunger, children are maimed from rat bites, women are dying of despair, and churches pass resolutions" (*Black Theology* 11). The remix of Cone's statement for the academy? Our classrooms are still not black and brown and indigenous enough; our students are still tracked out, dropped out, and stopped out; and our professional organizations pass resolutions.

In explaining how he arrived to these convictions, Cone says he came to link Christ and the Christian faith with the Black Power movement

> because I knew deep down that I could not repeat to a struggling Black community the doctrines of the faith as they had been interpreted by Barth, Bultmann, Niebuhr, and Tillich for European colonizers and white racists in the United States. I knew that before I could say anything meaningful about God and the Black situation of oppression in America I had to develop a theological identity that was accountable to the life, history, and culture of African American people. (*Black Theology* xiv)

All of Cone's writing is clear about the synthesis of Malcolm and Martin, civil rights and Black Power, that Black Theology was founded on. In accounting for how he perceived this synthesis in his 2000 book *Risks of Faith*, Cone says that King's contribution to Christianity—not just for black people but for the entire faith—"transformed our understanding of the Christian faith" by linking justice with love and rooting religious faith in practice in addressing what people are willing to do to make their faith real. Before King, Cone asserts, white supremacy and racial segregation were so widely accepted that almost no religious thinkers challenged these notions, or even wrote or talked about them. He says that after King, no one, not even Pat Robertson or Jerry Falwell, would publicly defend them. Cone argues, "That change is due almost single-handedly to the theological power of King's actions and words" (xvii). But Black Theology for Cone and the many other theologians who have contributed to its forty-plus-year history is not only "unapologetically Christian" but also "unashamedly Black," identified with black people and Black Power, completely aware of the depths of anti-black racism and the beauty, power, and possibility in black people. In describing Malcolm X's contribution to his own thinking and to Black Theology as a movement, Cone says:

> It is one thing to recognize that the gospel of Jesus demands justice in race relations and quite another to recognize that it demands that African Americans accept their Blackness and realize that I could never be who I was called to be until I embraced my African heritage—completely and enthusiastically. He taught me that a colorless Christianity is a joke—only found in the imaginary world of white theology. It is not found in the real world of white seminaries and churches. Nor is it found in Black churches. That Black people hate themselves is no accident of history. (xx)

So for black theologians during the intellectual, activist, and spiritual movement that is Black Theology, faith has been rooted in struggle, demanded a passionate response to racism, focused on black unity across denominational lines, emphasized black history and culture, challenged conservative black churches, and, later in its development, came to regard sexism, class oppression, and homophobia as crucial issues for action. Significant elements of this intersectionality came much later, as a result of challenge from and dialogue with feminist, womanist, and Third World theologians, and its central tenets can be summarized this way:

- The central message of the gospel and the Christian faith is not hope but liberation. Black theologians actively sought to disrupt the notion of religious faith as abstract and otherworldly to one that demands people's action right here, right now, on behalf of the oppressed.
- One must come to the experience of faith through the particular history and culture of a people. Black people cannot be liberated if they cannot be free to embrace their blackness fully, emphatically, lovingly.
- People must recognize the connections between related forms of oppression: we must understand that race, class, gender, and sexuality are related.
- One cannot recognize or embrace blackness or fully love himself or herself without looking to Africa and the rest of the diaspora.
- Faith demands self-criticism—people must be willing to look inward at their own contradictions and struggles, even as they look outward.
- One must unflinchingly confront the complexities and nuances of the difficult questions, but such nuance cannot silence one's passion or clarity of commitment.

As groundbreaking a movement as Black Theology was in the 1960s and 1970s because of Cone's polemics and balance of deep love and the sometimes agonistic rhetoric of Gayraud Wilmore, Cecil Cone, John Mbiti, and others, it would not stand as a mixtape movement, as a powerful example of synchronizing varied traditions and synthesizing dialectical tensions, if it were not for Katie Cannon. Nor would the movement stand as a powerful application of black griotic traditions to questions of a liberationist ethics. From the outset of her classic book *Katie's Canon: Womanism and the Soul of the Black Community*, Cannon makes it clear that she intends to disrupt the patterns and assumptions of both mainstream academic discourse and Black Theology. She includes at the very beginning of her preface her vision of her work as bringing a cannon to traditional academic discourse—boom! boom!—and as both creating canons and opening up canons in ways that make spaces for the voices and traditions of black women and, by extension, for all black people.

One of the most radical acts of canon formation and transformation that stands among Cannon's most significant contributions in shaping Womanist theology and changing Black Theology has been the establishment of black folk traditions and black women's literary traditions as both sources and norms for theology and ethics. Cannon created and pursued this reframing of theological work informed by Alice Walker's four-part definition of womanism, identifying her objective and the objective of womanist theology by using Walker's definition as "a critical, methodological framework for challenging inherited traditions for their collusion with androcentric patriarchy as well as a catalyst in overcoming oppressive situations through revolutionary acts of rebellion. My overall goal in this project is to recast the very terms and terrain of religious scholarship" (24).

This recasting of the terrain for Cannon originates in her own experience, in her own home. She begins with her mother's garden in North Carolina and the stories that she shared during violent thunderstorms. During these moments, the family literally disconnected, unplugging everything electrical, turned off all the lights, and came together in the stories her mother shared. Cannon's mother and her stories continued the work of her grandmother as a "gatekeeper to the land of counterpain" (24). The stories were far more than entertainment or renderings to pass time until the storms passed; for Cannon they were and are "the indispensable source of Black people's historical confidence and spiritual persistence despite all oppression. . . . These narratives are the soil where my inheritance from my mother's garden grew" (28). For a people whose history was tied to laws defining any act of distributing print material to black people a criminal act, Cannon's home and the oral tradition became a "folklore sanctuary." This counterculture, counterpain, not only allowed black people to survive the blight, to paraphrase her title for this chapter, but to reclaim their dignity and humanity, allowing people opportunities to strip away the social absurdity of chattelhood so carefully camouflaged in the dominant culture. In other words, folklore was the mask the slaves wore in order to indict slavery and to question the society in which it flourished. By objectifying their lives in folktales, Afro American slaves were able to assert the dignity of their own persons and the invincibility of their cause. (34)

Cannon's brilliance and innovation, however, came not just in choosing to locate her own life and work in the folk tradition but in her hacking of the methodological tools of theology and social ethics in the interests of liberation for black women and black people in ways similar to the technological appropriation accomplished by DJs in creating and circulating mixtapes, inserting black music and narrative in resistance to white-controlled media networks and conglomerates driven by predetermined formats, payola, and a willingness to circulate mainly or only those representations of black people that reified the worst stereotypes and upheld the established social order. To put it differently, Cannon's theoretical, methodological, and interpretive defiance rests in the determination to present black narrative and oral traditions as sources and norms for doing work as an ethicist. She makes the case for such a radical reorientation of theology and social ethics by noting that the stories and oral tradition shared in homes and hush harbors was intrinsically connected to prayer, and "hence I grew up understanding the Black prayer tradition to be the authentic living bridge between Black people's stories, Black people's music, and Black people's source of faith" (36).

Cannon makes the case for folklore and black women's literary traditions as sources and norms for work in ethics and theology by first unmasking the "hermeneutical distortions" and racist roots in the history of biblical exegesis, demonstrating that for centuries Western Christianity and these distortions "mythologized" black inferiority, enslavement, and divine will in the explicit interests of maintaining white supremacy. These patterns of interpretation have to be challenged and new canons created because these "same general schemes of oppression and patterns of enslavement remain today, and because the biblical hermeneutics of oppressive praxis is far from being dead among contemporary exegetes" (46). A womanist approach that recovers the "real-lived texture of Black life and the oral-aural cultural values implicitly passed on" and places black women and their literature and oral traditions passed down by women at the center of theological work is not about developing "any prescriptive or normative ethic" but about reclaiming agency and demonstrating

> how Black women live out a moral wisdom in their real-lived context that does not appeal to the fixed rules or absolute principles of the White-oriented, male-structured society. Black women's analysis and appraisal of what is right or wrong and good or bad develop out of the various coping mechanisms related to the conditions of their own cultural circumstances. In the face of this, Black women have justly regarded survival against tyrannical systems of triple oppression as a true sphere of moral life. (60)

In addition to making the case for black women's literature and folklore as sites for the construction of a womanist ethics, Cannon develops the details of one such understanding of ethics—again, not from the Bible but from the life and work of Zora Neale Hurston. The broad mandate of such an ethics is that "we are called to embrace a holistic justice agenda, casting our lot with the liberation of the darkest women of color" (72) through a commitment to Morrison's rememory, to developing "the emotional resources for dealing with forgotten memories that lie dormant in our bodies and therefore in our souls" (75). Hurston's life "incarnated a personality of harmonious complex opposites" (81), and her body of folklore and literary work "brings together a religion of opposites, and when these opposites are made to coincide, there is the power of new life" (84). There is no room for a false sense of moral perfection when confronting deeply rooted systems of oppression for Cannon, and the "ethical treatise" that emerges from her mixtape of Hurston's work and black folklore traditions presents three important elements:

- a primary focus on "surviving the continual struggle"
- finding virtue in the "interplay of contradictory opposites"

- balancing the nuances and complexities of those opposites "in such a way that suffering did not overwhelm and endurance with integrity was possible" (83)

Because of these commitments,

> in their tested and tried existential realities, the majority of these women refuse to get caught up in the gaudy accoutrements of the middle-strata sham. Against the vicissitudes of labor exploitation, sex discrimination, and racial cruelties, they embrace an ingenuity that allows them to fashion a set of values on their own terms as well as to master, radicalize, and sometimes destroy pervasive negative orientations imposed by the larger society. (83)

This ethical framework is very similar to some principles Tricia Rose identifies in our current digital moment. In *The Hip Hop Wars: What We Talk About When We Talk About Hip Hop—and Why It Matters*, her long-awaited follow-up to *Black Noise*, Rose mines Hip Hop's gardens with the same focus on working through complexity and binaries that Cannon elucidated in essays a quarter century earlier. Her conclusion identifies six principles she argues can be guiding principles for the Hip Hop generation as it navigates the difficult terrain between Hip Hop's brilliance, possibility, and well-documented problematics. Simplistic choices of acceptance or resistance are impossible, and often ill-advised, and she argues that those who hope to pursue progressive politics and community-building for black people and in dialogue with other communities can adopt the following as "guiding principles":

- Beware the manipulation of the funk.
- Remember what is amazing about chitterlings and what isn't.
- We live in a market economy; don't let the market economy live in us.
- "Represent" what you want, not just what is.
- Your enemies might be wrong, but that doesn't make you right.
- Don't settle for affirmative love alone; demand and give transformational love. (262)

Hurston represents a different model of ethics for Cannon, one that is not determined or structured by a Christian tradition that has often cared very little for black people, their concerns, or their struggle to end racism or the legacies of psychic, economic, educational, and medical pain still tied to racism. Black Theology as a mixtape movement and the creative work of the mixtape allow for a similar reconsideration of the ethical issues surrounding—and often defining the scope of—writing. There is an old joke among black church parishioners about churches that seem to exist only in order to raise money for the building fund, for buildings that never seem to get built. What happens to considerations of writing and ethics when compositionists worry less about our own building funds, about the limitations placed on us by administrations that don't seem to respect our disciplinary depth, or about whether our traditional service role contributes to such lack of respect? What happens when we move beyond questions of getting more faculty or TA lines, getting more sections, and securing more fair budgets and decide, along with Bradford Stull, that composition's primary job is an emancipatory one (or as Keith Gilyard would argue in this examination of Cornel West's influence on the field, a liberatory one)?

When it comes to questions of writing and teaching writing in a digital age, in some ways there is only one ethical question after we address the question of access, the role that writing and writing instruction continues to play in keeping our universities as homogenized as they still are—the question of how the writer, the teacher, and the theorist of writing will address intellectual property and copyright issues. And it is in dealing with this set of issues that we must return to Bernie Mac's question: "Who you wit?!?!?!" Just as Black Theology as a movement calls Christians to quit worrying about the building fund, stand clearly in solidarity with those who are oppressed and suffering, and "refuse to get caught up in the gaudy accoutrements of the middle-strata sham," the mixtape as Hip Hop art form calls compositionists to stand on the side of the wide range of different, everyday writing practices that have emerged from vernacular cultures into public awareness and into our students' conceptions of what it means to write. Will we stand with a set of codes, laws, and conventions that have pushed more and more severely in the direction of huge corporate interests, or will we stand with the interests of students and a public of everyday people who have clearly shown that mixing, remixing, and mixtaping result in new texts, new creations? Will we stand on the side of language policies and evaluation strategies that still dismiss the rich traditions students of color bring to the classroom, or will we accept the disingenuous argument that providing students the codes to succeed in corporate society is our only or most important goal?

I believe the mixtape as practiced not only by everyday music fans but by DJs like Bambaataa, Kid Capri, and many more calls composition to move beyond our own focus on the disciplinary building fund, calls us to completely rethink our stance toward access and toward copyright on all levels of our professional work: our approaches to citation practices, definitions of plagiarism, public conversations about what constitutes fair use, the kinds of assignments we create, and many more. In short, we need to adopt—or at least make theoretical and pedagogical space for—a copyleft stance toward practices like textual borrowing, photocopying, copying/pasting, patchwriting, collage, pastiche, mixing, remixing, and mixtaping.

And we're being hypocritical if we don't at least seriously consider pushing toward more open access to texts, images, sounds, and sites for the purposes of recontextualization and academic critique. No teacher can create any syllabus or teach anything without the explicit and implicit borrowing and reuse that DJs have celebrated and mastered. Every course we teach is a mixtape, a compilation of others' texts and ideas compiled, arranged, and combined with our own in various critical gestures we hope will inform and challenge our students. Every scholarly book or article we write is read as much for the selection, arrangement, mixing, and interpretative moves scholars brings to their engagement of other voices and ideas as for any brilliant, innovative—even original—argument or thesis they might forward. Every composition textbook implicitly plagiarizes in mixing together various theoretical and practical approaches handed down to us over the years of our experience and thrown into our own blender or mixer, selected and arranged based on our own priorities. And much of the time, even our own teaching on source use and citation and plagiarism itself is bootlegged, borrowed from various sources, often cited, sometimes not. Finally, the celebrated Kinko's case aside, every teacher and college professor in the country could be cited for violating the strict policies, ubiquitously posted in department offices and mailrooms, about photocopying texts for our students or ourselves.

When we consider the tensions and opposites that play out in the "tested and tried existential realities" around African American experience, it is easy to find that the mixtape and all of the assorted practices of the DJ are part of a much larger tradition of attitudes toward textual borrowing that have far more in common with the copyleft, Creative Commons, and open source movements than in corporate-lobbied contemporary versions of copyright law and intellectual property conventions. Lovalerie King develops this idea and describes some of the contours of this larger tradition in talking about textual borrowing practices and theft as theme in Frederick Douglass and Harriet Jacobs. She sets the context for her discussion by reminding readers that crime has been racialized and race has been criminalized in ways that target the practices of black people and defines them as somehow more threatening, more criminal, than other groups.

As a side note, I make a very similar point for my students all the time with respect to drug issues and the ways drug use is policed, punished, and taken up in our public discourse. I tell them to think about the ways drug use and drug crimes are reported to us, the ways we are inundated with messages from so many sources that the faces of our country's drug problems are black and brown, and primarily urban residents, and then to imagine that for a one-year period, the federal, state, and local offices and police departments that decide drug policy and punishment and the media that report these issues came to some agreement that the most pressing problem with drugs in our society was drug use on college campuses, from the sometimes professional job-holding alumni who run drugs back to their former campuses to the students who use them, and that every report from every media outlet and every discussion about the "problem" focused on the privileged, predominantly white middle- and upper-middle-class college students who are getting stoned and who can find any drug imaginable within minutes on any college campus. Sometimes my students return skeptical looks when I begin this kind of conversation with them. Then I ask them (and I have done this informally in at least ten of the courses I have taught over the last decade and a half) about various drugs: ecstasy, cocaine, heroin, marijuana, crack. For each drug, I ask how many of them could find each substance within an hour if they wanted, and usually 20–40 percent of them raise their hands. I follow up by asking how many of them know someone who could find each substance within an hour if they wanted to, and usually 50–75 percent say they can. The point? How we define crimes and "problem populations" matters.

Lovalerie King uses this larger point as it is developed in critical race theory and other scholarly spaces to talk about the ways "American legal and social practice contributed historically to the racialization of theft and unethical behavior in general and to the construction of the popular American image of the 'thievin negro,' in particular" (56). Her analysis of Jacobs and Douglas shows a different ethics at work, just as Cannon presents through Hurston a counterdiscourse challenging the racialized images of black people as thieves and criminals, explaining "'counter discourse' suggests more than a response or reaction to the dominant discourse driving negative stereotypes; it involves a preemptive strike, an overt action that anticipates a continuing future struggle" (King 56). Black authors have intentionally used their writing, she argues, to fight the dominance of this portrayal of black people. During American enslavement, because property and the right to own property were defined as belonging to whites and because black people were often forbidden by law from owning property, "the means to acquire it [for blacks] were necessarily defined as outside the law" (59). She proceeds to cite historians like Eugene Genovese to demonstrate that "whites, more often than not, attributed theft and stealing to *blackness* rather than to condition of servitude" (60). African American authors, from Frederick Douglass and Harriet Jacobs all the way through the tradition to Toni Morrison in the contemporary moment, work to counter the insidiousness of these stereotypes through calling attention to the legal and public discourses in which these assumptions operate, articulating a different ethical perspective related to theft, and offering different interpretations of events involving accusations of theft that often include details that complicate the alleged theft (60, 63). King also cites Douglass's argument that often theft, when it does occur, is necessitated by the desperate and inhumane conditions of servitude and dehumanization. Thus, in a system marked by oppression and domination, not all theft is a bad thing, as Douglass attests. This perspective also runs deep through the folktale tradition, especially in the case of the Br'er Rabbit tales, as Brother Rabbit is often shown pilfering food from gardens and plantations—as well as from other animals. A particularly pithy expression of this counterdiscourse about theft appears in the documentary *Wattstax*, where an older gentleman, filmed on his job in a work uniform (in other words, not a young man who might be judged as a "hood"), proclaims, "If I can't work and make it, I'll steal and take it."

Questions of countering narratives about theft are not just about physical property, however. Douglass often had to use "surreptitious means" to develop the literacy that led to his eventual freedom (King 63). When accused of theft, Douglass, Jacobs, Morrison, Richard Wright, and other writers boldly point out the hypocrisy of complicit members of a society built on the repeated, systemic, and legalized theft of the bodies, souls, minds, and culture of an entire people accusing any black person of anything (64, 71). In taking up King's analysis of the African American literary tradition and racialization of crime and theft onto black bodies, it is helpful to remember that long before the recording industry waged its wholesale campaign pursuing criminal and civil charges against college students and young people for the "theft" of music through peer-to-peer sites like Napster in the late 1990s, they trained their prosecutorial and persecutorial sights on Hip Hop DJs as thieves of intellectual property who needed to be punished. Legendary DJ Biz Markie was the target in what might be the most well known case of recording companies' pursuing this strategy. To bring the point about the "thieving Negro" stereotype to more contemporary intellectual property issues, *New*

York Times reporter Jayson Blair was thoroughly pilloried, made a national laughingstock, and scandalized to such an extent that his career was ended for having allegedly plagiarized quotes and articles, while *New York Times* columnist Maureen Dowd, also accused of plagiarism, still has a job and was never the mocked, scorned headline or punchline for a national conversation. Some scholars and everyday people still question whether Martin Luther King's use, borrowing, or plagiarism of sources taints his legacy, while presidential historians like Doris Kearns Goodwin are still employed, having recovered from a momentary scandal quite nicely: still paid, credibility still intact, easily repaired after those momentary difficulties. Biz Markie got sued, but Bob Dylan is a national hero.

Beyond the question of whether black people are still subject to old stereotypes or treated fairly in public conversation, black culture offers many examples of a different set of ethical principles in place with respect to "theft," borrowing, and reuse of both intellectual and material property. This other, different understanding, especially in the context of intellectual property battles, emerges from the black sermonic and storytelling traditions. There is an old joke about preachers and textual borrowing that goes something like this. The first time a preacher quotes someone, they might cite the text and the source—"As my good friend Reverend Walton preached a few months ago . . ."—and then proceed with the quote. The next time the preacher uses it, the original source might be masked, but it would still be attributed: "As a good friend of mine said some time ago . . ." The next time or any subsequent time, all references to having heard the quote are dropped, with it having become the preacher's own. Keith D. Miller describes the practices of textual borrowing and influence carefully, thoughtfully, and compellingly in his book *Voice of Deliverance: The Language of Martin Luther King, Jr., and Its Sources.* In showing the ways King borrowed significant portions of text from fellow preachers, from scholarship he read, and from advisors with whom he wrote collaboratively, Miller shows that there is something much more at work in King than mere plagiarism: a systematic, communal approach to textual appropriation that "embodies a system of knowledge and persuasion created by generations of Black folk preachers, including his father and grandfather. This system of voice merging enabled King to borrow sermons and skillfully intertwine his language and identity with those of his sources" (6). Thus, for Miller, the creative act does not consist solely in coming up with supposedly "original" text but rather in what one does with the sources one uses—how a person can take other material and make it his or her own, how one can develop a distinctive and compelling voice even through the voices of others.

It turns out that DJs and African American preachers have much in common with each other in their attitudes and grounding in this tradition, in articulating and practicing a communal system of textual production and knowledge-making built on a very different set of values and assumptions about what constitutes creativity from those programmed into contemporary (though, quite significantly, not the entire history of) American copyright law. Paul D. Miller aka DJ Spooky builds on Lawrence Lessig's well-known argument that "free content fuels innovation" (Miller 5). Miller argues that DJ culture is an archival, documentary one: "textual poaching" provides creative sparks for both unpaid labor and paid labor sold in the marketplace (12). He pushes even further to argue that DJ culture has laid a (not *the*, but *a*) foundation for networked Web culture: "I see the Web as a kind of legacy of the way that DJs look for information—it's a shareware world on the Web, and the migration of cultural values from one street to another is what this essay is about" (14).

Jonathan Lethem pushes Spooky's argument even further in his contribution to *Sound Unbound*, "The Ecstasy of Influence: A Plagiarism Mosaic." Lethem's essay demonstrates how, consciously and unconsciously, and at all levels of a text—theme, plot, argument, and specific language—we borrow and sometimes straight jack the stories, thoughts, and words of others. Building from such varied examples as Bob Dylan, Shakespeare, William S. Burroughs, Vladimir Nabokov, Muddy Waters, and animated series *The Simpsons* and linking his argument to debates over copyright going back to Thomas Jefferson's oft-quoted line "He who receives an idea from me, receives instruction himself without lessening mine; as he who lights his taper at mine, receives light without darkening me" (qtd. in Lethem 34), Lethem argues that "all art" uses such varied appropriation and that multilayered borrowing is central to acts of writing. Presenting an aesthetic based on the "beauty of second use" (35), Lethem's important contribution to this conversation is not necessarily from the actual claim that borrowing is central to the creative process or from his argument for an open-source approach to textual creation and copyright laws balanced more in favor of public domain and second uses of texts. These arguments have an important, if somewhat underground, audience. It's in the pitch or the particular voicing of the argument he brings to the conversation, the argument that such borrowing is *central* to the creative act: "It becomes apparent that appropriation, mimicry, quotation, allusion, and sublimated collaboration consist of a kind of sine qua non of the creative act, cutting across all forms and genres in the realm of cultural production" (29). After citing a line from *The Simpsons* that animation "is built on plagiarism" (29), Lethem walks readers through the debts many classic texts owe those before them—*Ren and Stimpy* could not exist without its writers jacking *Fritz the Cat*, we would have no *South Park* if it were not for Charlie Brown and no Simpsons without the Flintstones, no *Romeo and Juliet*, *West Side Story*, or *The Waste Land* without direct plagiarisms of Ovid and Plutarch.

After providing many examples of this kind of borrowing, from premise to plot or argument to specific phrasings and language, Lethem boldly proclaims, "If these are examples of plagiarism, then we want more plagiarism" (29). And he is right. His most important contribution, however, for my particular take on the mixtape as an act of vernacular canon formation, archiving, and aesthetic statement based on the explicit borrowing and mixing of various materials comes from his brief examination of a different ethic with respect to borrowing and appropriation to be found in black culture and specifically black music:

Blues and jazz musicians have long been enabled by a kind of "open source" culture, where preexisting melodic fragments and larger musical frameworks are freely reworked. Technology has only multiplied the possibilities; musicians have gained the power to *duplicate* sounds literally rather than simply approximate them through allusion. In 1970s Jamaica, King Tubby and Lee "Scratch" Perry deconstructed recorded music, using astonishingly primitive predigital hardware, creating what they called "versions." The recombinant nature of their means of production quickly spread to DJs in New York and London. Today an endless, gloriously impure, and fundamentally social process generates countless hours of music. (28)

Hip Hop, through the practices of its DJs—that lineage beginning with Kool Herc and Bambaataa and the thousands of professionals and amateurs all over the United States and now the world—made this open source culture and its argument for the "beauty of second use" explicit by openly and shamelessly producing, giving away, selling, and building their credibility upon the mixes, remixes, and mixtapes. They foregrounded the ways in which we all "interrogate the universe with scissors and a paste pot" (27), as Lethem describes William Burroughs's compositional practices, to such an extent that the cut and paste, the copy/paste, the sample, the loop, the remix, and the mixtape have become universally acknowledged and adopted practices—even when such acknowledgment and adoption have had to happen outside the gaze of legal systems and writing teachers dependent on Web sites like Turn It In to help them in their policing efforts. Because of old stereotypes of "thieving Negroes," these DJs and the culture they created bore the brunt of societal and legal disciplining and judgment when they should have been celebrated for offering us new ways into old debates that we have always engaged about copyright, about fair use, about intellectual property. The mixtape as practice is an example of Katie Cannon's demonstration that the vernacular and literary practices of black people often show us different interpretations of ethical questions, interpretations that are not dependent on the assumptions encoded into a culture that has always been dependent on theft. DJ culture and the mixtapes they created, gave away, and sold blatantly pointed out both the tensions in our long-standing debates and some of our old hypocrisies. Said to the recording industry, "Now if *that* ain't the pot calling the kettle black."

The importance of Cannon's mixtape, her theoretical and practical intervention, not only to Western theology but also to Black Theology, cannot be overstated. Just as James Cone notes in his book *Martin & Malcolm & America: A Dream or a Nightmare* that before Martin Luther King, no mainline academic theologian dared speak about, much less challenge, the role of the church and Western theology in upholding white supremacy, the same point holds for black male theologians before Cannon. None dared address sexism, sexuality, or gender oppression before Cannon and other womanist theologians. In Cone's 1984 book *For My People*, he offers regrets that he was so late in seeing the connections between racial oppression and sexism. Womanist theology stands not only as its own area but also as central to what Black Theology has become, as evidenced by introductions to the field written by both Dwight Hopkins and Diana L. Hayes. Cannon's theoretical, methodological, and interpretive wreck wielded in the interests of liberation for black women and all black people through her commitment to creating new canons that centralize the "real-lived texture of black experience" and transforming established canons to include and centralize those experiences shows us the progressive, even radical possibilities of the mixtape.

Accomplishing this possibility, however, requires far more of the mixtape than simply compiling, arranging, and distributing traditional and new narratives. These acts must be pursued in ways that link tradition and innovation and find value and wisdom in the everyday lives and experiences of black people and other groups—regardless of the rigidly stereotypical narratives that still circulate in mainstream society—and "call the question" on unequal systems of power, or as Cannon puts it in the title of one of her sermons, "calling for the order of the day." Black Theology as a mixtape movement that calls us to critically examine assumptions about what constitutes ethical living and the mixtape as a rhetorical form that reflects a different set of ethical assumptions about textual creation, borrowing, and appropriation can help "master, radicalize, and sometimes destroy" (Cannon, *Katie's Canon* 83) oppressive structures by grounding canon makers in their own communities and traditions even as they engage in dialogue with the broader society. It helps to answer Stull's call for an emancipatory composition because it moves us past rhetorical exemplars and into vernacular, communal practices and into greater agency for individual writers to engage with traditions and discourses on their own terms.

There are two important implications of the mixtape as Cannon demonstrates its theory and practice for digital and multimedia writing beyond those that I have noted so far. The mixtape as an act of intentional canon formation grounded in the griotic traditions of black people and the storytelling and folklore traditions of all people helps to address the generational tensions that I discussed in chapter 3 as hallmarks of black culture, and even the writing classroom in our digital age. It helps us develop pedagogy and praxis that link oral traditions, print literacies, and digital work explicitly. It helps us address Kamau Daáood's concern for young people who "refuse to wear the psychic beehive hat, / swarm of conceptual killer bees awaiting you on the world wide web," allowing them and us who are elders or slightly older to avoid the seduction of the trappings of the "middle-strata sham" even as we participate in and are often complicit in it. Cannon's work helps us understand how to synchronize the wide-ranging traditions and synthesize the conflicting positions that mark African American life—and American life—in this moment. Finally, it helps us address the difficulties imposed by the fact that the embrace of technologies means that we often give over more and more of our time and our lives to mediation by the practices and assumptions of huge corporate entities that have little regard for social justice or the quality of black life, even when they use notions of blackness to sell their tools and applications. The mixtape can help students to see, as Lethem argues, that

> finding one's voice isn't just an emptying and purifying oneself of the words of others but an adopting and embracing of

filiations, communities, and discourses. Inspiration could be called inhaling the memory of an act never experienced. Invention, it must be humbly admitted, does not consist in creating out of a void, but out of chaos. Any artist knows these truths, no matter how deeply he or she submerges that knowing. (29)

The embrace of those filiations and those communities can also help students maintain some balance between the individualistic, isolating effects of digital life and assumptions about writing, their hyper-mediated nature and social networks with real-world physical communities, between tradition and innovation. Between access and transformation.

SupaShouts: Diva Delight (www.divadelight.org) and Rootwork the Rootsblog: A Cyberhoodoo Webspace (http://rootsblog.typepad.com)

SupaShout: Diva Delight

This digital griot project is the blog of a DJ who goes by the name Princess TamTam who uses her Web space to document and pay respect to house music and club culture. The pseudonym Princess TamTam is homage to divas throughout black history, taken from Josephine Baker's 1935 film of the same name. More than simply a fan site, however, Princess TamTam brings the skills of the DJ to her blog, mixing, remixing, and mixtaping discourses to

enter these dialogues with an emphasis on the theoretical and analytical configurations of this music and culture. The Diva Delight website grew out of a growing interest in the creative technologies of computers and the cyber realm, democratizing voices, notions of otherness, diasporic travels, media activism and a generous curiosity. It is an interactive part of research on ethnographic methodologies, cultural capital, industries, and economies, queer theory, critical race and gender studies, cultural expressivities and modes of identification through distinct music texts. Although house music and club culture enjoys diverse audiences around in the world, a primary focus of Diva Delight is placed upon the assumed racialized and

so-called "non-normative" sexualities and genders in the historical
formation and subsequent relationships of particular communities
to house music and club cultures. (C. Mitchell, "Reconsidering" 8)

Diva Delight's work through the blog weaves technology and
narrative in order to create community as well as help envision new
possibilities for human agency while challenging, even rupturing,
hegemonic language and assumptions. The documentary impulse
of the blog is presented through sections on house music and house
divas, with other nodes introducing the site and building networks
and communities through the links, photos, and comment features
found on many blogs. Carmen Mitchell, aka Princess TamTam, in
her analysis of the site, identifies its purpose as a visual and textual
documentary project, a "diasporic Black feminist cultural project that
places the cultural lives of Black women into history" ("Reconsidering" 2). House music becomes an important space of engagement
not only for black women and the iconic figure of the "house diva"
but for globalization, sexuality, racialized identities, and what Robin
Kelley would call the freedom dreams of African Americans in their
wide-ranging identities and subjectivities. The blog's persona, Princess TamTam, through her grounding as a DJ, is committed to using
the site as an archive, a project in historiography, that centers the
stories, the narratives of black women, and her own self-narrative,
because those narratives offer kinds of knowledge that other quali-
tative or quantitative measures simply do not. Mitchell's analysis,
by working through theorists like Hortense Spillers and Patricia
Hill Collins, foregrounds the blog's intentionality around this issue:
"Privileged knowledges of the West, most particular, in the academy,
have been disseminated through the form of written texts. Hence, as
an African American woman and continuing graduate student, it has
been a priority to textually archive the 'subjugated knowledges' of
orature or oral cultures" (4). Thus, for Mitchell, and for her persona
Princess TamTam, multimedia writing allows for the reinsertion of
not only the narratives and experiences of black women but the
forms of knowledge and the epistemologies that emerge from the
oral tradition. These possibilities help to counter the erasure of black

women's experiences, histories, and the complex connections to be found in reading those experiences and histories diasporically.

One of the many functions TamTam fills in the blog is an ongoing questioning of subjectivity and knowledge construction in online spaces. TamTam pursued the blog as a way of doing intellectual work that she saw as lacking in the academy, as a response to limitations she saw in her own writing and research (Mitchell, "Reconsidering" 10). But Mitchell leads readers through some of the challenges involved in constructing knowledge:

> In the public cyberspace, I could talk about, center, and interview Black women house divas. Thinking back on it now, I actually did most of the interviews of the various house divas I featured on the Diva Delight website after I wrote my thesis! all too often these house divas are often heard on record and in dance clubs around the world but are hardly seen or given the opportunity to speak other than through vocal musicality. . . . I had a feeling that their voices might not get too far only stuffed in my thesis so the public space of the cyber world enabled me to circulate these stories beyond academic communities. (10, 11)

But Mitchell does not limit her analysis to this additional possibility presented by online forums for writing. She questions why she pursued these stories online, why she was willing to write about the black gay men who make up house culture in her master's thesis but not in the online space of Diva Delight: "I may have even been dealing with my own internalized homophobia by doing this. It was OK to center Black gay men in a text or a thesis but not online, especially coming from an uppity little Black chick in graduate school whose friends just happened to be gay men who liked house music" ("Reconsidering" 10). Mitchell also uses Judith Halberstam's challenge to those doing archival work to make their archives more than just a repository in ways that echo Manning Marable's demand that the work of the scholar be rooted in "passionate collective memory" (Marable, *Living Black History* 58). She notes that she wanted to make the archive and its stories live, bringing "users, interpreters, cultural historians to wade through the material and piece together a jigsaw puzzle of queer history in the making" (Halberstam qtd. in Mitchell,

"Reconsidering" 12). In her thoughtful analysis of her work through the site and its possibilities for griotic work, Mitchell concludes, "Despite these glaring inconsistencies with my past research that are almost shocking to me in hindsight, I hope that *Diva Delight* can be a space in which convergences of Blackness, womanhood and queerness can happen despite my own admitted limitations and areas of focus in cyberspace" (12). Mitchell's reflections on the challenges and possibilities of publicness, multimedia writing in online spaces, her own subjectivity, and her commitments to documenting parts of the black experience are rich and layered and help us counter the utopic/dystopic narratives about technology and black experience that Alondra Nelson challenges with Afrofuturism and Papa Legba.

SupaShout: Rootwork the Rootsblog: A Cyberhoodoo Webspace

Rootsblog also explicitly joins the oral tradition, print/essayistic literacy, and digital writing thematically, functionally, and aesthetically. The site's creator, novelist and storyteller Arthur Flowers, author of *Another Goodlovin Blues, De Mojo Blues: The Quest of Highjohn the Conqueror*, and *Mojo Risin: Confessions of a 21st Century Conjureman*, identifies himself on the Web site:

I am flowers of the delta clan flowers and the line of o killens
novelist, syr mfa fiction prof, organizer, performance poet,
mganga maua, babagriot of the hoodoo way
I fancy myself a visionary

The babagriot in the literary line of John Oliver Killens uses his Web log to "manifest" on current events, politics, black life and culture, world affairs, diasporic connections, his own writing process, and more and invokes figures from the folk tradition—Highjohn the Conqueror in particular—in order to do rootwork, or conjure, or use the magical powers of the word to speak truth, power, and healing into black communities in their ongoing journey. By explicitly linking conjuration to twenty-first-century realities, Rootwork announces its synthesis of contrasts and its synchronization of tradition and innovation from the very beginning, inviting its readers and larger community to join him in establishing the trunk, branches, and leaves of black identity and experience in a new age.

Highjohn the Conqueror, although not as well known as the Signfyin Monkey, Br'er Rabbit, Anansi, or Shine, is one of the major trickster figures of the black oral tradition and is celebrated because of his indomitable spirit and continual ability to outwit enslavers and others complicit in the oppression of black people. Referenced throughout African American literature and the blues tradition, from Zora Neale Hurston to Muddy Waters, John the Conqueror often possesses magical qualities and performs superhuman feats. Highjohn is one of the major figures revered by practitioners of Hoodoo, conjuration, or rootwork.

Flowers sees the oral tradition as a crucial element of the work that remains for black people in the pursuit of liberation and a better society for everyone, and he grounds his connection of tradition and futuristic vision in the same essay that frames Carmen Kynard's study of her students' digital writing practices. John Oliver Killens's 1972 essay "Wanted: Some Black Long Distance Runners" exhorts his literary and scholarly colleagues to look at the work of liberation and societal transformation as the work of generations. By comparing most activism in that current moment to sprints as opposed to marathons and supermarathons, Killens calls his readers and colleagues to construct fifty-year plans, hundred-year plans. Flowers sees his linking of technology and tradition as part of a response to Killens's call and sees his storytelling and literary and digital work all as parts of the challenge of using the power of the word to speak truth, healing, and power to his people in challenging them to continue the search for higher ground in the twenty-first century.

5

Fade: Notes toward an African American Rhetoric 2.0

> Innovation | vision | quality | tradition
> —replife aka Daniel Gray-Kontar, PhD student/DJ/MC

AND WE RETURN TO THE VERY BEGINNING, the initial invocation that launched this book project: DJing is writing, writing is DJing. Paul Miller's statement, important fort both its clarity and reciprocity in the copula and the flip—DJing is not like writing, writing is not similar to DJing, each *is* the other—calls us to consider what the DJ offers to conceptions of writing when we move beyond a few mentions of individual writing practices completely lifted from context, from tradition, from social, cultural, political, and technological networks. When the DJ is viewed as a crucial component of a griotic tradition and linked to other griots in the forms of storytellers, preachers, standup comics, and everyday people, practices like the mix, remix, and mixtape push beyond general postmodern free-floating signifiers and begin to suggest, yes, exciting writing practices, but practices linked to principles, priorities, and purposes for understanding the complexities of writing in a multimedia age.

When I was invited to be one of the visiting scholars at Ohio State University's digital media and composition seminar a couple of years ago, I was asked my take on the differences between some of the various terms used to describe the intersection of writing and digital technologies: computers and writing, new media, digital writing, multimedia writing. I wandered, somewhat clumsily, through the question at the time, attempting to avoid some of the political issues attendant in the various terms and the different visions of what writing instruction should be that were loaded in or onto them. I wish I had not been so circumspect in that moment, as watching some of these debates unfold (as departments or programs attempt to decide what they name themselves and individual scholars position their work) has demonstrated even more clearly than I might have realized then just how important academic nomenclature can be. The saturation of digital, networked technologies in our culture and in the education system means many changes for what we think of as writing, but for me the most important of those changes is not the information literacy argument, as we have always talked about information literacy as central to the education process. It is not the technological tools themselves, as every era introduces different tools, systems, and ways of knowing and thinking about technologies that demand that we shift our attitudes toward writing and communication. The most important issue in this particular convergence of digital, networked technologies and writing or composition is the fact that composing in everyday and academic contexts is far more multimedia and multimodal than it has been at other times in our history (although rhetoric and composition's history has many reminders that notions of the oral and visual have always been a part of our conceptions of writing on some level).

Beyond the changes that we have witnessed in composing practices, processes, and products over the last two decades, however, the rise and saturation of digital technologies and the narratives about their importance that have emerged and even become hegemonic lead me to believe that writing in this multimedia age must be more than multimodal, more than multimedia: it must be a digital humanities project—in other words, intellectual work connecting technologies, in all the layered senses in which we use the word, to humanistic inquiry. Acts of writing, the social networks and cultural contexts in which they occur, and the technological networks in which they take place and are disseminated still involve systems of power, still reflect the relationships between individuals and groups within those systems, and still entail questions of what it means to be and how we come to see, hear, sense, and know the world with all of those technologies, power relations, social networks, and cultural contexts.

I have attempted to argue in this book that African American oral traditions, understood particularly from the perspective of the figure of the griot, offer writers, teachers, and scholars powerful ways to link oral performance, print literacies, and digital technologies in a truly multimedia approach to writing. On the level of purpose, or exigence, black griotic traditions call for an approach to writing that is committed to the range and flexibility to "teach in the idiom of the people" and committed to writing as not just remix but as rememory, or the passionate collective memory to which Manning Marable calls scholars. These traditions also call writers to something larger and more important than mainstream notions of success, to a commitment to long-term work and struggle with the difficult questions and issues an individual, community, or society might face. In terms of principles, the digital griot demonstrates a synthesis of deep, searching (crate-digging) knowledge of the traditions and cultures of his or her community and futuristic vision; the skills, ability, and comfort level to produce in multiple modalities; the ability to employ those skills toward the purpose of building and serving communities with which he or she is aligned; an awareness of the complex and layered ethical commitments and questions facing that community; and the ability to "move the crowd," to use those traditions and technologies for the purposes of persuasion.

By moving beyond specific practices and into a broader conception of the purposes, principles, and priorities that the digital griot, seen as an important part of a broader griotic tradition, offers understandings of writing in a multimedia age, we see that the DJ and the tropes of mix, remix, and mixtape provide a place from which to begin the work of reimagining African American rhetoric as a field of study in a new century. Therefore, a second (implied) argument throughout this book has been that we must imagine an African American rhetoric 2.0, as a digital humanities project, as a thorough linking of texts, techne, and technologies in the examination of how black people have engaged in the techno-dialogic, or the mutually constitutive relationships that endure between humans and their technologies.

The beauty of the remix as trope is that in its focus on renewed vision, on re-vision, those doing the remixing never discard the original text. The antecedent remains an important part of the next text, the next movement; ancestors and elders remain clear, and even central, to the future text. This is the way I view the relationship between an African American rhetoric 2.0 that I want to see scholars and students flesh out and the definitions and articulations of African American rhetoric that we have in place today. Let me call up a few of those definitions as I make an argument for a new mix, remix, and mixtape for this field of inquiry:

> [African American rhetoric is the] study of culturally and discursively produced knowledge-forms, communication practices, and persuasive strategies rooted in freedom struggles of people of African Ancestry in America. (Richardson and Jackson xiii)

> Black discourses have been the major means by which people of African descent in the American colonies and subsequent republic have asserted their collective humanity in the face of an enduring White supremacy and have tried to persuade, cajole, and gain acceptance for ideas relative to Black survival and Black liberation. (Gilyard, "Introduction," 1)

> Hush Harbor rhetoric is composed of the rhetorics and commonplaces emerging from those rhetorics, articulating distinctive social epistemologies and subjectivities of African Americans and directed toward predominantly Black audiences in formal and informal Black publics or African American centered cultural geographies. (Nunley 221)

> African American rhetoric is the set of traditions of discursive practices—verbal, visual, textual, performative, digital—used by individuals and groups of African Americans toward the ends of full participation in American society on their own terms. These traditions and practices have both public and private dimensions and embrace communicative efforts directed

at African Americans and at other groups in the society: hence, directly persuasive public address and less overtly persuasive day to day performances that contribute to the creation of group identities are all viable subjects of African American rhetorical study." (Banks 2)

Jacqueline Jones Royster, in her foreword to Elaine Richardson and Ronald Jackson's anthology *African American Rhetoric(s): Interdisciplinary Perspectives*, describes the definition Richardson and Jackson present in language that really applies to all of the articulations above:

They centralize the use of cultural frameworks in rhetorical analysis as they emphasize the importance of the practices that they are showcasing having emerged from people with a particular ancestry—African. They focus on discursive forms, which underscores the importance of verbality and rationality, rather than just orality and literacy. They acknowledge persuasion as the abiding purpose of interactive engagement within and across communities, and they make clear that the mandate that is quite compelling in these discursive forms is tied unequivocally to struggles for freedom among this group. What's more, they present this view as part of knowledge-making processes, rather than as simply expressive traditions, suggesting that there are consequences for language use in terms of the ways that we think, act, and consider ourselves in the world. (ix)

All of these definitions work for me as continuing definitions of African American rhetoric as an area of study, even as I am pushing here for scholars to limn out this area of study as a fully developed digital humanities project moving forward. It would be rather easy to say that an African American rhetoric 2.0 means taking the definitional work of Gilyard, Royster, Richardson, and Jackson and applying it to digital means and spaces. By calling for a remixed conception of the field, however, I mean far more than scholars asking, "What are blackfolk doing online?" I also mean something richer than the American Council of Learned Societies describes in its 2006 report, *Our Cultural Commonwealth*, in its articulation of digital humanities

as a project that "cultivates leadership in support of cyberinfrastructure" and "encourages digital scholarship."

A revised vision of African American rhetoric as a digital humanities project for me certainly means rich, thorough examinations of
African American discourse in technologized and online spaces and
developing infrastructure and digital scholarship. But for me, those
goals just scratch the surface. I'm interested in what Joel Dinerstein
and Alex Weheliye identify as black survival technologies and a black
techno-dialogic. How have "African Americans created the nation's
survival technology" (Dinerstein 22)? How have black people imagined and reimagined what it means to be in relationship with ever-
changing technological landscapes? Landscapes where, as Johndan
Johnson-Eilola argues in his book *Datacloud*, large-scale changes
are difficult to document in the ways we are used to (by charting
history-making major or cataclysmic events) because the accumula-
tion of many interconnected small changes over long periods of time
leads to wholesale change we often don't recognize until we are fully
enmeshed in them. I hope to see scholars and students explore the
complicated ways in which micro- and macro-level technological
developments in American society affect African American life and
the discursive production that emerges from those moments.

The role of Hip Hop offers just one example, one metaphor, that
shows how we might reimagine our work with Alondra Nelson's
and Afrofuturism's synchronizing project in mind. Generation 2.0
of African American rhetoric scholars has done amazing work using Hip Hop primarily through the figure of the rapper or MC to
explain black discursive practices, launched needed debates about
representation, interrogated systems of power and privilege, and
created space in the writing classroom for black bodies and their
languages to be respected. An African American rhetoric 2.0 would
continue that work and still have love for the MC but begin with
the DJ and link digital technologies and practices and processes and
all their attendant issues to the questions it raises and the answers
it finds. African American rhetoric 2.0 should still examine issues
of representation and language in the lyrics of black music, but, as
Barbara Garrity-Blake does with fish chanteys in her essay "Raising

Fish with a Song: Technology, Chanteys, and African Americans in the Atlantic Menhaden Industry," it would examine prison songs, work songs, and field hollers as powerful examples of techne and "invisible technology" that not only made labor, like laying railroad track and menhaden fishing, possible but fueled the larger American technological enterprise and "signified . . . expressed resistance to white authority, freedom" (114) and built community and shared the worldviews of black people in those communities. A couple more examples of the differences I mean might be illustrative here. The famous debates between Booker T. Washington and W. E. B. Du Bois about the scope and goals of education for black people was just as much about the transition from an agrarian to an industrial age as it was about "skills" versus/with "critical literacies." African American rhetoric 2.0 would continue to examine this debate but would also begin to ask how everyday discursive practices and broader attempts to move the people were rooted in the realities of how technological change affected and affects black life, individual and communal identities, discourse, and persuasive efforts. Ben Williams's masterful examination of the history of techno music in Detroit in the 1980s provides another example. In his essay "Black Secret Technology," he describes the emergence of techno music in terms of the sonic and intellectual influences on the music and also the story of how Juan Atkins and other legendary techno DJs used technologies to create a new form of music. In addition, Williams documents how techno's history was deeply rooted in, and was a direct response to, the relationships between race, technology, class, and labor that marked the United States and post-industrial Detroit.

Bold, creative, innovative uses of technologies; deep inquiry into technologies' influences on African American lives and African American influences on technologies; African American survival technologies across eras; digital scholarship; development of cyberinfrastructure for studying black texts and discourses—all of these and more are crucial to the development of African American rhetoric as a twenty-first-century discipline that thoroughly values and thoroughly weaves together spoken, oral, visual, and digital means of persuasion. By isolating the mix, remix, and mixtapes as tropes for reimagining African American rhetoric and its links to composition, I have suggested that training writers to be digital griots can help them develop skill and expertise in oral, print, and digital modes of presentation in ways that promote an ability to build from one's own cultures and traditions even as writers enter ever-changing cultural and digital spaces.

Beyond synchronizing and bringing more critical attention to the relationships between technologies, oral traditions, print, and multimedia writing, however, an even greater task for an African American rhetoric 2.0 is in synthesizing the many poles and continua that mark black rhetorical production and academic work:

- old school/new school—tradition and innovation
- Saturday night and Sunday morning: street and church, secular and sacred
- Malcolm X's focus on black communities and Martin Luther King Jr.'s aims for a broader, transformed Beloved Community
- the block and the rock—a commitment to addressing local, national, and transnational issues
- specificities in black experiences and issues and searing intersectional interrogation and critique of sexism, racism, class, and sex oppression
- radical democracy and black nationalisms
- public discourse and vernacular traditions/practices in the underground
- disciplinary and interdisciplinary concerns

By advocating synchronizing and synthesis as theoretical goals for the study of African American rhetoric, I'm in no way suggesting that the tensions in these areas can or should be "resolved" by scholarly attention to them, even though my own rhetorical move, if you will, is to search for moments and traditions of synthesis in and amid what seem to be dichotomies. Instead, I mean that we should look to examine the poles of the polemics together. Therefore, regardless of one's own inclination for, say, Malcolm over Martin or jazz over Hip Hop or religious rhetoric over the secular, I am arguing here for a conception of what it means to study African American rhetoric that demands that students in this area be exposed to the polemics and the continua in the tradition in such a way that they understand that there is no such thing as a "pure integrationist" or a "pure nationalist," as Manning Marable and Leith Mullings note, or that one cannot appreciate King without knowing X, as James Cone teaches, or that P-Funk gets sampled in gospel music just like it does in Hip Hop, and that even public rhetoric by blackfolk often still has yet other layers of meaning in the underground—just as arguments and discursive patterns that have their roots and intended audiences in the underground, whether by design or appropriation, can always find their way into public, mainstream discourse.

Beyond the argument for such an approach, however, questions remain: What does it mean to take the abilities and practices of the griot in African American culture and put them to use in digital writing and activism? What does it look like to teach students in school and out to become like Papa LaBas and to have that approach define how they view writing with technologies and in the ever-changing environment that marks writing in digital spaces? The combination of the many griotic figures in African American culture—the storytellers, the preachers, the everyday griots in their recreations of history and future, the DJs—offers us both a set of abilities and skills in addition to the framework for an outlook that allows us to see writing as serving local communities as well as the official purposes we assign writing in schools and workplaces. This framework includes an understanding of writing and technology as tools to preserve cultures even while planning future agendas; a focus on technologies as tools for reform, resistance, and renewal—as possible elements of a progressive politics of transformation; a set of ethical commitments that requires us to confront systems of oppression and exploitation in solidarity with those who have been systematically excluded from our society; the ability to produce in multiple modalities and to understand the conventions, possibilities, and constraints of various modalities; a deep and searching understanding of the traditions and cultures of one's community; and a rhetorical focus on being able to move the crowd, which requires (among other things) an ability and willingness to speak across the continua or tensions that mark a particular community at a particular time.

The specific projects shouted out through the text—digNubia, Cyber-Church, Arthur Flowers's Rootsblog, Diva Delight, and Marcyliena Morgan's Hiphop Archive—show digital griots at work, using digital writing and technologies to build and sustain community through flow, layering, and rupture. Scholars like Carmen Kynard and Elaine Richardson demonstrate uses of technologies toward liberationist pedagogies building from and through Tricia Rose's concepts of flow, layering, and rupture. As they point the way forward, Katie Cannon and James Cone, everyday griots, keep us moving forward by keeping us connected to traditions, to "surviving the blight" and engaging in creative struggle against those external constraints still on people's lives while maintaining dignity in the midst of the madness. Reimagining the work ahead, for me, means understanding that writing changed in the Bronx in 1973: completely rooted in the tradition and opening up possibilities that few, if any, saw besides the DJ. African American rhetoric in 2010 and beyond finds itself in a new era defined by amazing new possibilities and brutal realities that its study can help elucidate, in ways that few other areas can, if it proceeds committed to community, linking the truths and discursive practices found in oral traditions to rigorous analysis of the relationships between society and its technologies.

There are voices on the scholarly scene to show us what these relationships can look like, as well. Richardson's important volume *Hip Hop Literacies* provides an important spotlight for those of us wading into new literacies waters, with analysis of wide-ranging literate practices from poetry to beat-making to video gaming, and Jon Yasim makes valuable contributions for scholars looking to build pedagogical bridges between young people, Hip Hop culture, writing, and technology. Dara Byrne and Tyrone Taborn, with essays published in Anna Everett's volume *Learning Race and Ethnicity*, also begin to point the way to scholarly agendas for the future. Taborn's "Separating Race and Technology: Finding Tomorrow's IT Progress in the Past" points to the cultural dimensions at work between race and technology when youth in all strata of our society idolize

Kobe Bryant but have never heard of Dr. Mark Dean, the black engineer who played crucial roles with IBM in the development of the personal computer. He reminds us again that histories, current circumstances, and future visions are all linked and challenges us to continue to work for real, meaningful technology access: "Saying that the Digital Divide is closing because minorities have greater access to computers is like saying minorities have a stake in the automobile industry because they drive cars" (39). Taborn calls us to mine the pasts of African American achievement in science and technology to destroy thoroughly the myths of black disinterest in science, technology, engineering, and math fields and introduces the concept of "cyber mentoring" to bring African American and other students of color fully into digital networks.

Byrne's essay "The Future of (the) Race: Identity, Discourse, and the Rise of Computer-Mediated Public Spheres" is an ambitious study of more than three thousand discussion threads on the early social networking sites BlackPlanet, MiGente, and Asian Avenue in order to better understand the relationships that endure between rhetorical production and racial and ethnic identities in online spaces. Her analysis helps us see that social networking sites and other digital spaces that adults might dismiss as insignificant are potentially powerful vehicles for civic engagement (32) and that regardless of our views of young people's interests or discourse, we must understand the contours of the conversation as they see it, if there is to be any potential for community-building or connecting with young people. Similarly, there is much that we can do in order to see that youth understand that "there is a fundamental relationship between collective voice and social change" (32).

Taken together, Taborn's and Byrne's articles push us to think more carefully about how rhetoric and technology might be brought together in both scholarship and collective action. We need major, detailed studies of how African Americans from many different social locations are using social networking tools like SecondLife, Facebook, Twitter, and LinkedIn, and the particular flavors and valences they bring to technology convergence. We need students and scholars following up on important developments black people have brought to e-government conversations: how should people organize to use digital tools to have better access to and influence on policy debates, budgetary processes, and dialogue with government officials? We need to extend Royster's and Shirley Wilson Logan's examinations of the lyceums that sparked nineteenth-century social movements to see if and where such spaces exist online and what kinds of rhetorical principles black people are learning in them. We need careful, thoughtful exploration of ways Juneteenth and Pullman porters and black women's organizations developed and maintained social and activist information networks in order to see what we might learn from them and apply to today's scholarship on network theory. And we need many studies detailing precisely how black students, scholars, and laypeople use technologies in the writing process—the strategies they employ, the tools they use, the assumptions they bring to writing tasks, the ways they engage with digital interfaces in order to begin conversations with human-computer interaction. We need to pay careful attention to the many episodes of digital activism in which African Americans are engaged as well as they ways they are using digital tools to participate in movements that black people are not usually associated with, like environmental justice. And maybe most of all, we need painstaking digital documentation and preservation of African American stories, sayings, oral histories, proverbs, toasts, jokes, and other oral texts across generations in order to have a fuller historical record preserved as we continue to develop new bodies of folklore.

African American rhetoric 2.0 must build a strong focus on study-ing and changing the relationships that endure between race, ethnic-ity, culture, rhetoric, and technologized spaces. The generation of scholars that has entered the academy since "Writing in the Spaces Left" has a critical opportunity to help reshape both African Ameri-can rhetoric and all of composition studies by mixing, remixing, and mixtaping these intersections. Theoretically, this means an im-perative to "noisily bring together competing and complementary beats without sublimating their tensions," as Weheliye reminds us (13). Ethically, it is a call to identify whom and what we are here to serve, willing to stand not only with black people but also with others who still struggle against oppression. Pedagogically, it means a firm commitment to build from the truths and tropes of black experience in writing curricula, courses, assignments, evaluation, feedback, and teacher stance and delivery—not just for black students but as a part of the education all students receive. It means building assignments that invite students not only to work across modalities but also to link those multiple modalities, individual assignments, and assignment cycles and in critical examination of the power relations and material conditions inscribed in technological tools, networks, and discourses. Practically, it means working to increase meaningful, transformative access to digital technologies for people on their own terms. It means mix, remix, mixtape. Access and transformation. Healing, celebration, self-examination, and critique. Community. Flow, layering, rupture. Innovation, vision, quality, tradition. Afrodigitized. Word.

WORKS CITED
INDEX

WORKS CITED

Alkalimat, Abdul. Cyber-Church. Accessed August 2008. <http://www.cyber-church.us>.

Alkalimat, Abdul, et al. "eBlack: The Next Movement in Black Studies." eBlack Studies. February 21, 2000. Accessed March 3, 2010. <http://www.eblackstudies.org/workshop/manifesto.html>.

American Council of Learned Societies. Our Cultural Commonwealth: The Report of the American Council of Learned Societies Commission on Cyberinfrastructure for the Humanities and Social Sciences. 2006. Accessed March 3, 2010. <http://www.acls.org/uploadedFiles/Publications/Programs/ Our_Cultural_Commonwealth.pdf>.

Anderson, Daniel. "The Low Bridge to High Benefits: Entry Level Multimedia, Literacies, and Motivation." Computers and Composition 25.1 (2008): 40–60.

Banks, Adam J. Race, Rhetoric, and Technology: Searching for Higher Ground. Mahwah, NJ: NCTE/Erlbaum, 2006.

Barlow, William. Voice Over: The Making of Black Radio. Philadelphia: Temple, 1998.

Bigger and Blacker. Dir. Keith Truesdale. Perf. Chris Rock. 3 Art Entertainment, 1999.

Brathwaite, Fred, aka Fab 5 Freddy. Introduction. Back in the Days. By Jamel Shabazz. New York: Powerhouse, 2001. 6–9.

Brooke, Collin. Lingua Franca: Toward a Rhetoric of New Media. Cresskill, NJ: Hampton, 2009.

Brown Sugar. Dir. Rick Famuwiya. Perf. Taye Diggs, Sanaa Lathan, and Mos Def. Evergreen Productions, 2002.

Byrne, Dara. "The Future of (the) Race: Identity, Discourse, and the Rise of Computer-Mediated Public Spheres." Learning Race and Ethnicity: Youth and Digital Media. Ed. Anna Everett. Cambridge: MIT, 2007. 15–38.

Cannon, Katie. "Calling for the Order of the Day." Keeping the Faith: African American Sermons of Liberation. Ed. James Haskins. New York: Welcome Rain, 2002. 113–23.

————. Katie's Canon: Womanism and the Soul of the Black Community. New York: Continuum, 1995.

————. Personal interview. March 17, 2007.

Cardenas, Diana. "Creating an Identity: Personal, Academic, and Civic Literacies." Latino/a Discourses: Language, Identity, and Literacy Education. Ed. Michelle Hall Kells, Valerie Balester, and Victor Villanueva. New York: Boynton/Cook, 2004. 114–27.

Car Wash. Dir. Michael Schultz. Perf. Franklin Ajaye, Richard Pryor, and Antonio Fargas. Universal Pictures, 1976.

Coachman, Dale. Interview with Questlove. Waxpoetics 33 (2009): 32–35.

Condit, Celeste. "The Character of 'History' in Rhetoric and Cultural Studies." At the Intersection: Cultural Studies and Rhetorical Studies. Ed. Thomas Rostek. New York: Guilford, 1999. 168–85.

Cone, James. Black Theology and Black Power. Maryknoll, NY: Orbis, 1969.

————. For My People: Black Theology and the Black Church. Maryknoll, NY: Orbis, 1984.

————. Martin & Malcolm & America: A Dream or a Nightmare. Maryknoll, NY: Orbis, 1991.

————. Risks of Faith. Boston: Beacon, 2000.

————. The Spirituals and the Blues: An Interpretation. Maryknoll, NY: Orbis, 1972.

Coogan, David. "Community Literacy as Civic Dialogue." Community Literacy 1.1 (Fall 2006): 96–108.

Cook, William. "Writing in the Spaces Left." CCC 44.1 (1993): 9–25.

Cushman, Ellen. The Struggle and the Tools: Oral and Literate Strategies in an Inner City Community. Albany: State U of New York P, 1998.

Daáood, Kamau. "Blakey's Drumsticks." The Language of Saxophones: Selected Poems of Kamau Daáood. San Francisco: City Lights, 2005. 85.

Dance, Daryl Cumber, ed. From My People: 400 Years of African American Folklore. New York: Norton, 2003.

Davis, Ossie. Purlie Victorious: A Comedy in Three Acts. Hollywood: Samuel French Plays, 1961.

digNubia. Accessed August 2008. <http://www.dignubia.org>.

Dinerstein, Joel. Swinging the Machine: Modernity, Technology, and African American Culture between the World Wars. Amherst: U of Massachusetts P, 2003.

Do The Right Thing. Dir. Spike Lee. Perf. Spike Lee, Bill Nunn, and Joie Lee. 40 Acres and a Mule Productions, 1989.

Dyson, Michael Eric. Mercy, Mercy Me: The Art, Loves, and Demons of Marvin Gaye. New York: Basic Civitas, 2005.

———. "We Never Were What We Used to Be: The Politics of Black Nostalgia." Race Rules: Navigating the Color Line. New York: Vintage, 1997.

Ellison, Ralph. Shadow and Act. New York: Random House, 1953.

Fanon, Frantz. The Wretched of the Earth. New York: Grove Press, 2004.

Flowers, Arthur. Rootwork the Rootsblog: A Cyberhoodoo Webspace. Accessed March 12, 2009. <http://rootsblog.typepad.com/about.html>.

Garrity-Blake, Barbara. "Raising Fish with a Song: Technology, Chanteys, and African Americans in the Atlantic Menhaden Industry." Technology and African Americans: Needs and Opportunities for Study. Ed. Bruce Sinclair. Cambridge: MIT, 2006. 107–18.

Gates, Henry Louis. The Signifying Monkey: A Theory of African American Literature. London: Oxford, 1989.

Gilyard, Keith. "Introduction: Aspects of African American Rhetoric as a Field." African American Rhetoric(s): Interdisciplinary Perspectives. Ed. Elaine Richardson and Ronald Jackson. Carbondale: Southern Illinois UP, 2007. 1-20.

———. Voices of the Self: A Study of Language Competence. Detroit: Wayne State UP, 1991.

Glaude, Eddie. In a Shade of Blue: Pragmatism and the Politics of Black America. Chicago: U of Chicago P, 2008.

Golden, Ean. "Mix Master." Remix Magazine, January 2009: 48.

Grabill, Jeff. Community Literacy Programs and the Politics of Change. Albany: State U of New York P, 2001.

Grace, Columbus M. "A Case Study of African American Students' Engagement Responses to Oral-Based Literacy Instruction: The Oral Narrative Engagement (ONE) Approach." Diss. Syracuse University, 2002.

Gramsci, Antonio. Selections from the Prison Notebooks. New York: International, 2008.

Hale, Tom. Griots and Griottes: Masters of Words and Music. Bloomington: Indiana UP, 1999.

Hayes, Diana L. And Still We Rise: An Introduction to Black Theology. Mahwah, NJ: Paulist, 1996.

Higgins, Lorraine, Elenore Long, and Linda Flower. "Community Literacy: A Rhetorical Model for Personal and Public Inquiry." Community Literacy Journal 1.1 (2006): 9–44.

Hopkins, Dwight. Introducing Black Theology. Maryknoll, NY: Orbis, 2001.

Hughes, Langston. "The Negro Speaks of Rivers." The Collected Poems of Langston Hughes. New York: Vintage Books, 1995. 23.

Johnson, James Weldon. God's Trombones: Seven Negro Sermons in Verse. New York: Penguin Classics, 2008.

Johnson-Eilola, Johndan. Datacloud: Toward a New Theory of Online Work. Cresskill, NJ: Hampton, 2005.

Johnson-Eilola, Johndan, and Stuart Selber. "Plagiarism, Originality, Assemblage." Computers and Composition 24.4 (2007): 275–403.

King, Lovalerie. "Counterdiscourses on the Racialization of Theft and Morality in Douglass's 1845 Narrative and Jacobs's Incidents." MELUS 28.4 (Winter 2003): 54–82.

Kouyate, D'Jimo. "The Role of the Griot." Talk That Talk: An Anthology of African American Storytelling. Ed. Linda Goss. Clearwater, FL: Touchstone, 1989. 179–81.

Kynard, Carmen. "Wanted: Some Black Long Distance Writers: Blackboard Flava Flavin and Other AfroDigital Experiences in the Classroom." Computers and Composition 24.3 (2007): 329–45.

Latterell, Catherine. Home page. Aug. 31, 2005. Accessed July 23, 2010. http://www.personal.psu.edu/cxl40/.

Latterell, Catherine. Remix: Reading and Composing Culture. New York: Bedford/St. Martins, 2005.

Lethem, Jonathan. "The Ecstasy of Influence: A Plagiarism Mosaic." Sound Unbound: Sampling Digital Music and Culture. Cambridge: MIT P, 2008. 25–52.

Love Jones. Dir. Theodore Witcher. Perf. Nia Long, Larenz Tate, and Lisa Nicole Carson. Addis Wexler Pictures, 1997.

Lunsford, Andrea. "Writing, Technologies, and the Fifth Canon." Computers and Composition 23.2 (2006): 169–77.

Mao, Jeff "Chairman," with Afrika Bambaataa. "You Spin Me Round (Like a Record, Baby)." Vibe History of Hip Hop. Ed. Alan Light. New York: Three Rivers, 1999. 69–78.

Marable, Manning. The Great Wells of Democracy: The Meaning of Race in American Life. New York: Basic Civitas, 2003.

———. Living Black History: How Reimagining the African-American Past Can Remake America's Racial Future. New York: Basic Civitas, 2006.

Marable, Manning, and Leith Mullings, eds. Let Nobody Turn Us Around: Voices of Resistance, Reform, and Renewal. Lanham, MD: Rowman and Littlefield, 2000.

Medina, Tony, Samiya A. Bashir, and Quarishi Ali Lansana. Role Call: A Generational Anthology of Social and Political Black Art and Literature. Chicago: Third World, 2002.

Micaller, Ken. "A Healing Thing." Remix Magazine, January 2009: 23–24.

Miller, Keith D. Voice of Deliverance: The Language of Martin Luther King, Jr., and Its Sources. New York: Free Press, 1992.

Miller, Paul D. Rhythm Science. Cambridge: MIT, 2004.

Mitchell, Carmen. Diva Delight. Accessed August 2008. <http://www.divadelight.org>.

———. "Reconsidering Princess TamTam's Diva Delight: An Explanatory and Analytic Narrative." Unpublished essay.

Mitchell, Henry H. Black Preaching. Philadelphia: Lippincott, 1970.

Morgan, Marcyliena, et al. The Hip Hop Archive. Accessed March 2009. <http://www.hiphoparchive.org>.

Morrison, Toni. Beloved. New York: Vintage, 1988.

Moss, Beverly. A Community Text Arises: A Literate Text and a Literacy Tradition in African American Churches. Cresskill, NJ: Hampton, 2003.

National Committee of Black Churchmen. "Black Power Statement." New York Times, July 31, 1965.

Navas, Eduardo. "Remix Defined." Remix Theory. Accessed December 2008. <http://remixtheory.net>.

Neal, Mark Anthony. What the Music Said: Black Popular Music and Black Public Culture. London: Routledge, 1998.

Nelson, Alondra. "Future Texts." Afrofuturism: A Special Issue of Social Text. Ed. Alondra Nelson. Raleigh: Duke, 2002. 1–15.

Nunley, Vorris. "From the Harbor to Da Academic Hood: Hush Harbors and an African American Rhetorical Tradition." African American Rhetoric(s): Interdisciplinary Perspectives. Ed. Elaine Richardson and Ronald Jackson. Carbondale: Southern Illinois UP, 2007. 221–35.

Obama, Barack. "A More Perfect Union." Speech. Philadelphia, PA. March 18, 2008.

The Original Kings of Comedy. Dir. Spike Lee. Perf. Steve Harvey, Cedric the Entertainer, D. L. Hughley, and Bernie Mac. 40 Acres and a Mule Productions, 2000.

Parliament-Funkadelic. The Mothership Connection. Casablanca Records, 1975.

Pough, Gwendolyn D. Check It While I Wreck It: Black Womanhood, Hip-Hop Culture, and the Public Sphere. Boston: Northeastern UP, 2004.

Powell, Annette Harris. "Access(ing) Habits, Attitudes, and Engagements: Re-thinking Access as Practice." Computers and Composition 24.1 (2007): 16–35.

Reid, Alex. "Geoffrey Sirc @ Computers and Writing." Blog. Accessed March 3, 2010. <http://www.alex-reid.net/2007/05/geoffrey_sirc_c.html>.

———. "Portable Composition: iTunes University and Networked Peda-
gogies." Computers and Composition 25.1 (2008): 61–78.
Rice, Jeff. "The 1963 Hip Hop Machine: Hip Hop Pedagogy as Composi-
tion." CCC 54.3 (2003): 453–71.
———. The Rhetoric of Cool: Composition Studies and New Media
Carbondale: Southern Illinois UP, 2007.
Richardson, Elaine. Hip Hop Literacies. London: Routledge, 2006.
Richardson, Elaine, and Ronald Jackson. African American Rhetoric(s):
Interdisciplinary Perspectives. Carbondale: Southern Illinois UP, 2007.
Robinson, Beverly. "Historical Arenas of African American Storytelling."
Talk That Talk: An Anthology of African American Storytelling. Ed.
Linda Goss. Clearwater, FL: Touchstone, 1989. 211–16.
Rose, Tricia. Black Noise: Rap Music and Black Culture in Contemporary
America. Middletown, CT: Wesleyan, 1994.
———. The Hip Hop Wars: What We Talk About When We Talk About
Hip Hop—and Why It Matters. New York: Basic Civitas, 2008.
Rose, Tricia, with Beth Coleman. "Sound Effects." Technicolor: Race,
Technology, and Everyday Life. Ed. Alondra Nelson. New York: New
York UP, 2001. 142–53.
Royster, Jacqueline Jones. Traces of a Stream: Literacy and Social Change
among African American Women. Pittsburgh: U of Pittsburgh P, 2000.
———. "When the First Voice You Hear Is Not Your Own." CCC 47.1
(1996): 29–40.
Run DMC. "King of Rock." Raising Hell. Profile/Arista, 1986.
School Daze. Dir. Spike Lee. Perf. Laurence Fishburne. 40 Acres and a
Mule Productions, 1988.
Selfe, Cynthia, and Gail Hawisher. Literate Lives in the Information Age.
Mahwah, NJ: Erlbaum, 2004.
"Shine and the Titanic." From My People: 400 Years of African American
Folklore. Ed. Daryl Cumber Dance. New York: Norton, 2003. 488.
Sinclair, Bruce. "Integrating the Histories of Race and Technology." Tech-
nology and the African-American Experience: Needs and Opportu-
nities for Study. Ed. Bruce Sinclair. Cambridge: MIT P, 2006. 1–18.
Sirc, Geoffrey. Lecture. Computers and Writing Conference. Detroit.
May 17, 2007.
Smitherman, Geneva. "The Blacker the Berry, the Sweeter the Juice."
Talkin That Talk: Language, Education, and African Americans. Ed.
Geneva Smitherman. New York: Routledge, 1999. 163–94.
———. Talkin and Testifyin: The Language of Black America. 1977.
Detroit: Wayne State UP, 1986.

"State of Black America 2006." Tavis Smiley Productions. DVD, 2006.

"State of Black America 2007." Tavis Smiley Productions. DVD, 2007.

Stull, Bradford T. Amid the Fall, Dreaming of Eden: Du Bois, King, Malcolm X, and Emancipatory Composition. Carbondale, IL: Southern Illinois UP, 1999.

Taborn, Tyrone. "Separating Race and Technology: Finding Tomorrow's IT Progress in the Past." Learning Race and Ethnicity: Youth and Digital Media. Ed. Anna Everett. Cambridge: MIT P, 2007. 39–60.

Tyson, Timothy. Radio Free Dixie: Robert F. Williams and the Roots of Black Power. Chapel Hill: U of North Carolina P, 2004.

Van Sertima, Ivan. "Trickster: The Revolutionary Hero." Talk That Talk: An Anthology of African American Storytelling. Ed. Linda Goss. Clearwater, FL: Touchstone, 1989. 103–12.

Vie, Stephanie. "Digital Divide 2.0: 'Generation M' and Online Social Networking Sites in the Composition Classroom." Computers and Composition 25.1 (2008): 9–23.

Villanueva, Victor. Bootstraps: An American Academic of Color. Urbana: NCTE, 2003.

Warnick, Barbara. Rhetoric Online: Persuasion and Politics on the World Wide Web. New York: Peter Lang, 2007.

Wattstax. Dir. Mel Stuart. Warner Home Video, 2004.

Weheliye, Alexander G. Phonographies: Sonic Grooves in Afro-Modernity. Durham: Duke UP, 2005.

Werner, Craig. Higher Ground: Stevie Wonder, Aretha Franklin, Curtis Mayfield, and the Rise and Fall of American Soul. New York: Crown, 2005.

Wiggins, William. "The Black Preacher as Storyteller." Talk That Talk: An Anthology of African American Storytelling. Ed. Linda Goss. Clearwater, FL: Touchstone, 1989. 209–11.

Williams, Ben. "Black Secret Technology: Detroit Techno and the Information Age." Technicolor: Race, Technology, and Everyday Life. Ed. Alondra Nelson and Thuy Linh N. Tu, with Alicia Headlam Hines. New York: New York UP, 2001. 154–76.

Williams, Gilbert. Legendary Pioneers of Black Radio. Santa Barbara, CA: Praeger, 1998.

Woodson, Carter G. The Miseducation of the Negro. 1933. New York: Classic House, 2008.

Yancey, Kathleen Blake. "Redesigning Graduate Education in Composition and Rhetoric: The Use of Remix as Concept, Material, and Method." Computers and Composition 26.1 (2009): 4–12.

INDEX

Adam J. Banks is associate professor of writing, rhetoric, and digital media at the University of Kentucky and the author of *Race, Rhetoric, and Technology: Searching for Higher Ground.*

CCCC STUDIES IN WRITING & RHETORIC

Edited by Joseph Harris, Duke University

The aim of the CCCC Studies in Writing & Rhetoric (SWR) series is to influence how writing gets taught at the college level. The methods of studies vary from the critical to historical to linguistic to ethnographic, and their authors draw on work in various fields that inform composition—including rhetoric, communication, education, discourse analysis, psychology, cultural studies, and literature. Their focuses are similarly diverse—ranging from individual writers and teachers, to classrooms and communities and curricula, to analyses of the social, political, and material contexts of writing and its teaching. Still, all SWR volumes try in some way to inform the practice of writing students, teachers, or administrators. Their approach is synthetic, their style concise and pointed. Complete manuscripts run from 40,000 to 50,000 words, or about 150 to 200 pages. Authors should imagine their work in the hands of writing teachers as well as on library shelves.

SWR was one of the first scholarly book series to focus on the teaching of writing. It was established in 1980 by the Conference on College Composition and Communication (CCCC) to promote research in the emerging field of writing studies. Since its inception, the series has been copublished by Southern Illinois University Press. As the field has grown, the research sponsored by SWR has continued to articulate the commitment of CCCC to supporting the work of writing teachers as reflective practitioners and intellectuals. For a list of previous SWR books, see the SWR link on the SIU Press website at www.siu.edu/~siupress.

We are eager to identify influential work in writing and rhetoric as it emerges. We thus ask authors to send us project proposals that clearly situate their work in the field and show how they aim to redirect our ongoing conversations about writing and its teaching. Proposals should include an overview of the project, a brief annotated table of contents, and a sample chapter. They should not exceed 10,000 words.

To submit a proposal or to contact the series editor, please go to http://uwp.aas.duke.edu/cccc/swr/.

OTHER BOOKS IN THE CCCC STUDIES IN WRITING & RHETORIC SERIES